Changing Aims in Religious Education

Changing Aims in Religious Education

by Edwin Cox
Lecturer in Education,
University of Birmingham

LONDON

ROUTLEDGE AND KEGAN PAUL
NEW YORK: THE HUMANITIES PRESS

First published 1966
by Routledge and Kegan Paul Ltd
Broadway House, 68-74 Carter Lane
London, E.C.4

Printed in Great Britain
by Northumberland Press Limited
Gateshead on Tyne

Contents

APR 3 1968

General editor's introduction

The Education Act of 1944 made collective worship and religious instruction in accordance with an agreed syllabus obligatory in both county and voluntary schools; no other aspect of the curriculum was so specified in the Act. This certainly marked the end of a long stormy period in English education when the 'religious problem' seemed obstinately insoluble; but did it in the long run do a service or a disservice to the cause of religious education? Mr. Cox's forthright and lively book makes a valuable contribution to this debate and it will be welcomed by students and teachers who want to think or rethink the matter through. His main concern is that whatever is done in the name of religious education should be in some fundamental sense both religious and educative.

J.W.T.

Preface

It is the aim of this book to look at the present situation of Religious Education as a whole, to consider the influence on it of current ideas in theology and educational psychology, and then to discuss what reasonable and realisable aims a teacher of the subject can set before himself, and the methods by which he may hope to achieve those aims. I am conscious that in doing this I have raised more problems than I have solved, but I hope that I have indicated the field in which the solutions may possibly be sought and found. Those whose approach is more traditionally based than mine will doubtless find many points of disagreement and even of alarm. But I ask that they credit me with no polemic intention, and regard what is written as a contribution to the debate about the future form of Religious Education, and judge it on its merits.

It is possible to discern at this time two distinct attitudes to Religious Education among those who are sympathetic to it. The more conservative one, which received general acceptance until fairly recently, regards it as a particular aspect of the Christian Churches' work of evangelism, aiming to transmit to the next generation the body of mixed knowledge and belief that is usually called 'Christian teaching', and to enrol pupils into one of the denominations of the Church. Many teachers still consciously and overtly pursue such an end, with varying degrees of success. But there is a growing feeling among those actively engaged in teaching that religious education of this type is just 'not on', except with a few children, who are already within a Christian body. The religious doubts and scepticisms of the adult world, they argue, are reproduced in the thoughts of schoolchildren once they are beyond the Primary School age, and if the religious teacher is to make any contact with and impact upon his pupils, his aims must be somewhat different from what they have been in the past.

Just what the new aims of the subject ought to be is not yet clear, but certainly in trying to define them we must take into account the new theological expressions that are emerging, and making some appeal to our more thoughtful contemporaries, and also the information provided by psychological research as to how religious concepts are formed in growing minds. Further there is a mounting conviction that if Religious Education is to continue in schools it must show that it has genuinely educational values, and allows children to learn through examination of their experience, and be guided, as in other subjects, to an interpretation of it, rather than have an interpretation imposed externally on that experience.

Any writer must be conscious of his debt to those who have previously published in his field. I am grateful to those whose writings have contributed to the ideas I have tried to set out. Their influence is acknowledged in as far as I have been conscious of it. In particular I should like

4

to thank Dr. K. E. Hyde for permission to summarise the general implications of the research which he did into the religious attitudes of schoolchildren, and Dr. R. J. Goldman, who gave similar permission with regard to his work and kindly read the relevant chapter and suggested many corrections and improvements. If I have, through brevity or misunderstanding, made any misrepresentation, or if I have been guilty of unacknowledged borrowing, I hope I may be forgiven. And for any errors or misjudgments that may be found the reader must blame only my own 'negligences and ignorances'.

E.C.

1

The legal position and its assumptions

No subject is easy to teach, but some are harder than others. Perhaps the most difficult of all at the present time is that which is known as Religious Education or Religious Instruction. Those who try to teach it find their task complicated, partly by the nature of the subject itself, and partly by the confusion as to the nature and value of theological ideas which is a characteristic of contemporary thought.

The teacher of mathematics can be confident of the facts he transmits. Provided he keeps within the bounds of conventional arithmetic, three times three will always make nine, and if any member of the class calls this in question a simple practical demonstration will quickly produce assent. Outside the classroom the community as a whole recognises the universally accepted truth of $3 \times 3 = 9$. Further it is admitted that to teach such truths to children is of value, since the knowledge will help them to deal with practical problems involving calculations and measurements.

The teacher of religion, however, has none of these

advantages. Religion, being the individual's reaction to the mystery of life and creation and his attempts to solve its most inscrutable problems by answers which must be largely symbolical and metaphorical, appears, by its very nature, to have no demonstrable facts. It belongs to the realm of feelings, values, judgments and opinions. The respect for toleration and freedom of conscience which has emerged in the last few centuries demands that all religious ideas, no matter how irresponsible or ill-informed, shall be regarded as equally valid. Unless the teacher is prepared to be more authoritative and dogmatic than is generally acceptable it may seem that he has no agreed corpus of fact to teach. Since most teachers of the subject are themselves religious to a degree, a great number of them feel justified in invoking some measure of authority. The past experience of the human race has, they argue, produced certain religious ideas which are universally valid. The more deeply committed of them would maintain moreover that certain truths have been disclosed by God through revelation, and that the Bible contains the more important of those truths. Consequently they feel justified in teaching facts about the origin and content of the Bible, and the history of religious ideas and religious behaviour. These are the facts of the subject, not totally dissimilar from the facts of arithmetic or geography. Since this view depends on the personal religious conviction of the person who holds it, not everyone in the community will agree with it, but will regard the ideas that form the material of religious education not as facts but as opinions which are demonstrably unprovable. What is more, some parents question the value of teaching them. Religion has so little practical influence on present day life, that they think the time might be better used in teaching a more utilitarian subject, while a small minority, who call themselves humanists or agnostics or atheists, think that religious ideas are definitely harmful and impede the development of the self-reliance proper to humankind.

The effect of this may be to make the teacher of religion feel he is alienated somewhat from parents, colleagues and pupils. Children absorb unconsciously the values of society and their attitude to the subject reflects the doubt in which it is generally held. Those who come from religious families and attend public worship may be keenly interested but the remainder have neither the interest nor the motivation to study the subject with enthusiasm. Teachers of other subjects can be either politely tolerant or openly hostile, though often they are genuinely sympathetic without feeling competent to express more than a vague benevolence. In such a situation those who undertake religious education may feel that they have a difficult and lonely furrow to plough, and it is necessary for them to think carefully of the rationale of the subject, of the nature of its material and its aims, and of how closely its methods can approximate to those of subjects about which there is more widespread agreement.

Despite doubts of its validity and value, R.E. is the only subject that must by law be included in the curriculum of all schools within the state education system, and this provision would seem to claim the support of the majority of parents. In an investigation conducted by the writer in 1963, 2,278 parents of sixth form Grammar School pupils were asked whether they supported regular religious instruction in schools. Of the 74.5% who answered, only 89 were opposed leaving 69.5% in favour. Wider evidence comes from a survey in *New Society*, 27th May, 1965, which found 90% of the adult population of Great Britain in favour of the existing arrangements. It may be that those who oppose R.E. are a smallish intellectual group, the sort who are capable of writing letters to the more responsible papers and whose vocal influence is disproportionate to their size. It may be that most parents wish to see the subject retained, partly because its removal would imply a repudiation of the religious view of life which, for all their doubts and indifference, they are not prepared to make, and partly because they feel that it has some useful influence on moral training. Certainly any attempt to modify the religious provisions of the 1944 Education Act would provoke considerable opposition, and not only from churchgoers.

THE 1944 (BUTLER) EDUCATION ACT

The 1944 Education Act made religious instruction and religious observance a legally required ingredient of school life:

> The school day in every county school and in every voluntary school shall begin with collective worship on the part of all pupils in attendance at the school, and arrangements made therefor shall provide for a single act of worship attended by all such pupils, unless . . . the school premises are such as to make it impracticable to assemble them for that purpose. (section 25.1)
>
> Religious instruction shall be given in every county school and in every voluntary school. (section 25.2)

In the detailed provisions of how these instructions are to be carried out, and in allowing abstentions therefrom, the Act takes into account the different types of school, the wishes and beliefs of the parents, and the conscience of the teachers. Strangely no reference is made to the wishes of the pupils in this matter, although one must remember that in 1944 the school leaving age was 14, and elder pupils did not claim the freedom to choose their beliefs and actions as extensively as they do today. It will perhaps be convenient if we examine these provisions under the headings of schools, parents and teachers.

(a) The schools. These are divided into three types, according to their origin and religious tradition, with different provisions for each. There are firstly the county schools, i.e. those provided and entirely maintained by the local authority. These have no religious tradition or affiliation, and in them both the instruction and the opening act of worship is independent of any denominational influence. The instruction is based on an agreed syllabus which the local authority has either drawn up for itself or adopted from another authority. Secondly, there are the controlled voluntary schools. These originally belonged to some other body, usually one of the churches, but have now become financially the complete responsibility of the local education authority. Consequently these retain a little of their original religious colouring. The former owners can be represented on the managing body, and two periods a week of the appropriate denominational instruction may be given to those children whose parents wish it. If the school is large enough, the teaching staff may include persons especially competent to give that instruction, who are known as 'reserved teachers'. Though appointments are made by the local authority, the managers have the right to assure themselves that 'reserved teachers' are suitable for the task, and, if any prove to be otherwise, may ask the authority to dismiss him. Apart from these two periods a week, all religious instruction has to be undenomina-

tional and within the scope of an agreed syllabus. Thirdly, there are the 'aided' voluntary schools. The management retains control of religious education in these and of the appointment of the teachers, in return for which the Act stipulated that they pay 50% (reduced to 25% in 1959) of the cost of keeping up the exterior fabric of the building and of any alterations. The local authority pays the whole of the running costs. For practical purposes these remain denominational schools under church control, though parents of pupils may request that their children be taught according to an agreed syllabus—a request that in fact is rarely made.

(b) The parents. It is a principle of the religious provisions of the Act that parents have the right to decide what sort of religious instruction their children shall receive. Since it is not always possible for children to attend a school giving the desired type of instruction, provision is made for withdrawal and for alternative teaching. Parents who have no belief may therefore ask that their children be exempted from all religious instruction and from the daily act of worship. As mentioned above, those whose children attend voluntary-aided schools where denominational teaching is general, may request undenominational agreed syllabus instruction. Those whose children attend a county or controlled school, but none the less wish them to be taught according to a denominational formula, may withdraw them at either the beginning or end of school to receive such teaching, provided it can adequately be given elsewhere. This means the alternative teaching must be provided by a church at its own cost and in its own building.

Apart from the Roman Catholics, parents in general are

strongly disinclined to make use of these facilities. Either they are unaware of them, or indifferent to the type of religious instruction their children are given, or, more probably, content to leave this, as they leave other educational decisions, to the schools on the grounds that 'they know best what is good for children'.

(c) The teachers. It is expected, of course, that teachers in aided schools and reserved teachers in controlled schools will be religious people, acceptable to the managers who watch over the religious life of the school. But with these exceptions the Act states in section 30 that no teacher shall be required to give religious instruction, and that none shall 'receive any less emolument or be deprived of, or disqualified for, any promotion' for feeling unable to do so. Nor shall his private opinion or his abstention from the daily act of worship penalise him in any way. Yet teachers frequently accept an assignment to give religious teaching who would prefer not to do so. They do this partly because they recognise the problems of constructing and manning a timetable, and do not wish to cause difficulties for their school, and partly because they feel the legal provisions are a little disingenuous, and that the giving of religious instruction can be regarded as a qualification for promotion. After all, the head of a school has to be responsible for arranging religious instruction and for providing the daily act of worship, and not unnaturally, some appointing committees prefer candidates who can do this with enthusiasm and skill. There is a feeling among teachers that heads tend to be chosen from those with religious conviction, although the writer would not care to say whether this impression is true or false.

THE AGREED SYLLABUSES AND THEIR PRESUPPOSITIONS

The production and use of an agreed syllabus in each area was fundamental to the success of the religious provisions of the 1944 Education Act. The introduction of legally required religious instruction in all state schools would have been impossible in the early part of the twentieth century because of the bitter denominational rivalries and suspicion that then existed. But by the time the Act was drafted the churches had grown sufficiently close together for them to be able to co-operate in the drafting of such syllabuses, and to welcome their use in schools as imparting a useful background of common knowledge without doing damage to any denominational interest. It is to the agreed syllabuses that one must look to discover the principles on which religious instruction under the Act has been conducted and the assumptions on which it is based.

Certain agreed syllabuses already existed when the Act became law. For instance the Cambridgeshire syllabus had been published in 1924 and adopted by more than three hundred authorities. But after 1944 many authorities drew up their own syllabuses while some were content to adopt those of other authorities, the ones of Cambridgeshire, Surrey and Sunderland being widely used. The authorities that made their own syllabuses appointed drafting committees which included theologians, representatives of the different churches, and members of teacher's associations and the local authority. In retrospect it may appear that the theological and ecclesiastical influence predominated, and that too little account was taken of the teaching situation in which the syllabus was to be used, and too little known of the manner in which children's attitudes and religious ideas develop. This is not a reflection on the sincerity or integrity of the drafting committees. They had to work within the knowledge then available. None the less, the opinion now exists that their syllabuses, though excellent schemes of theological and biblical study for those already interested in such things, are in need of revision to relate them more closely to children's needs, and the present time is seeing a number of revisions.

The criticism now directed at agreed syllabuses may be in part due to a misunderstanding of their nature by teachers and their consequent misuse. They were intended to be syllabuses, not lesson schemes. This is made clear in the preamble to many of them. The *London Agreed Syllabus of Religious Instruction* (1947) states that 'It cannot be overstressed that the syllabus is intended to be suggestive rather than compulsory' (p. 29). The introductions to the *Surrey County Council Syllabus of Religious Instruction* (1947) contain this advice: 'It remains for the teacher to select and arrange such courses as will be suitable for the organisation and other conditions in the individual school. . . . It is for the individual teachers, working within the comprehensive school plan, to interpret and shape the content of the courses' (pp 7, 31). This means that the agreed syllabus defines the material that may be taught. How it is taught, when it is taught, and in what order it is taught, is for the teacher to decide. The syllabus describes the area in which the teacher may manoeuvre in the manner which seems to him most profitable. Provided the material he is using can be found somewhere in the syllabus, he is within his rights. This has perhaps been obscured by the arrangement of the syllabuses into infant, junior and senior sections, and further subdivisions into years. Such arrangement gives the impression that the syllabus is a scheme of lessons and some teachers, either through lack of imagination or initiative or from fear of going beyond their brief, have used it as such, instead of drawing up their own lesson plan based on the material that the syllabus defines. It can, therefore, be argued that the agreed syllabuses, so misunderstood, have had a restrictive effect on the teaching of the subject far greater than was envisaged by those who compiled them.

To understand fully the influence that the agreed syllabuses have had on religious instruction one must realise their presuppositions—the things which they take for granted. The following assumptions seem to have been made by their compilers:

1. That when the Act refers to religious instruction it means instruction in the Christian religion. The word Christian does not appear in the text of the Act, yet all the syllabuses are based on a study of the Christian scriptures and the history of the Christian Church, and this is beyond doubt what the legislators intended.

2. That every child is a Christian and comes from a Christian home. This further implies that all children are anxious to learn the details of Christian faith and practice, and will readily accept these when they are expounded. There is no suggestion that these may be a matter of choice to the children, or that they may be one method among others of explaining their experience. Apart from occasional sections for seniors, such as that in the Surrey syllabus headed 'Problems of religion and life' the syllabuses do not take an apologetic point of view, or imply that the children may have to be persuaded to accept the beliefs as well as learn what they are. The practical outcome of this is

that the teaching can easily appear to be indoctrination rather than education.

3. That the view of the nature of theological truth which was acceptable before the rise of scientific thought is still valid. God is regarded as a material creator, standing outside his creation, but watching over it and occasionally intruding to modify it in the form of a miracle. He has made his will known by a series of revelations, and obedience to his commands form the basis of the moral code. Thus religion is seen as a collection of accepted propositions to be transmitted, rather than as a vital reaction to the mystery of life. This again reinforces the temptation to make religious instruction the authoritarian propounding of dogma rather than an experimental search for meaning.

4. That the Bible is the unquestioned source book of Christian belief and that to learn its contents will of itself have a beneficial effect on character and produce religious faith. Not unnaturally Bible study takes a large place in the syllabuses, since it comprises a collection of stories, poems, and aphorisms which were not only acceptable to all denominations but which could easily be turned into lesson material. Little thought, however, appears to have been given to the likely reaction of the pupils to the Bible material. It was assumed they would accept it, more or less at its literal value, and respond to it in a Christian way. Thus the syllabuses take little account of the critical and historical approach to the Bible that has long been orthodox in scholarly theological writing (though not in the popular exposition of Christianity in churches) or of the fact that the appeal and meaning of the Bible may be different for those who have a

Christian background than for those who have not. The latter may reject the authority of the Bible or question the literal veracity of its contents, but the syllabuses do not allow for this.

5. That children of all ages think about religion in the same way. Most of the experimental investigations into the manner in which religious concepts develop, and the age at which children are able to acquire them, is of comparatively recent date. The compilers of the agreed syllabuses now generally in use did not have the advantage of their findings. Consequently the syllabuses presuppose that children's religious thinking becomes deeper and more complex with age without changing in quality. Little attempt is made to grade the narrative stories of the Bible according to the maturity of religious understanding they demand. The same story is sometimes introduced at different ages in the hope that the pupils will understand it in greater detail and find new meanings in it each time it is told. In fact, as we now know, the stories may have totally different meanings for children of different ages, and, if introduced at the wrong time, may convey a teaching quite different from that which is intended. Further, wrong understanding of a story, through its too early use, may preclude a right understanding of it at a later age.

Such has been the organisation and assumptions of religious organisation in England for the past twenty-one years. How far has it succeeded? There is a growing feeling that it has achieved far less than was hoped. Certainly if we measure its success by the number of active Christians it has produced there is some justification for this feeling. Church statistics show that the number attending public worship has not significantly increased, nor is there evidence that the traditional Christian moral standards are being widely observed. A report, *Religious Education in Secondary Schools*, produced by the Sheffield University Institute of Education in 1961 showed that even the simpler ideas taught in the scripture lesson were not being retained for any long period by most children. An investigation in the same field conducted by the Institute of Christian Education and written up in 1961 by Harold Loukes under the title *Teenage Religion* concluded that religious thinking among pupils in secondary modern school pupils is confused and inarticulate. 'These fourteen-year olds are interested in religious issues. . . . Not only these specific enquiries into religious interests but the most general studies of adolescent attitudes would also indicate a readiness to take religion seriously. . . . Despite their high concern and the integrity of their point of view, these young people show little sign of a constructive framework of thought and intelligible belief. They have a site, but no house', (pp. 90-3). A more popular appraisal of the effect of religious instruction by Diana Dewar in *Backward Christian soldiers* (1964) concludes:

> the variety and scope of the religious influences conspire to complicate the problem of finding suitable answers to the needs of young children. It is plain, however, that the present solutions are not the right ones. Agnostics can describe the situation as 'not too bad' because it is inefficient; and from the religious standpoint much of our teaching can be seen to be making too small an image of God and to be giving children ridiculous ideas. (p. 121)

If these strictures be true, what has gone wrong with the subject? It may be that the intentions of the Act have not been implemented, and there are schools where, through indifference or incompetence, the subject is less well taught. On the other hand much care has been expended on training teachers of the highest devotion and no little skill. The failure seems to lie not so much in the integrity and methods of the teachers as in the rejection by the children of the teaching now being given. It conveys the wrong impression and fails to satisfy their needs. Have the aims been wrong? Have the assumptions behind the teaching been in error? Have the general attitudes to religion and the belief of the community so much changed since 1944 that by continuing to use old methods and old syllabuses teachers are trying to deal with a situation that no longer exists?

2

The theological and social background

One of the less obvious assumptions of the agreed syllabuses mentioned in the previous chapter was that all children were Christian, came from Christian homes and would react in a Christian manner to their religious instruction. Yet it is apparent that throughout this century Christianity in its traditional form has steadily lost its hold on the thoughts of great numbers of people. That is not necessarily to say they have become less religious, but rather that the thought-forms and observances through which religious feelings formerly expressed themselves no longer seem adequate for that purpose.

In this retreat from Christianity practice preceded theory. Its first outward manifestation was a decline in attendance at public worship. Men began to stay away from church because there were other occupations which seemed of greater interest or importance. This is another way of saying that what went on in church seemed no longer vital or meaningful to them. Next, Christian practices began to disappear from everyday life. How far Bible reading and family and private prayers declined is difficult to estimate since there is little real evidence of how widely they were previously practised. Certainly things began to be done on Sundays which would not have been countenanced before, even by those not noted for their piety, until that day has become distinguished from the others more for its recreational than its religious quality. Yet, because practice preceded theory, these things were done with an uneasy conscience. Individuals often expressed the wish that they read the Bible more, or said their prayers more frequently or 'found time' to go to church more often. They were uneasy rebels and attributed their apostasy to lack of will rather than to its real cause, which was change of conviction.

In the past twenty years men have become more conscious of the ideas that have influenced this modification of their religious behaviour. Those who have remained content within the Christian scheme would say that this is a rationalisation of a wish to sin, but this is too superficial a description of the situation. Rather it is a realisation that certain elements have entered into human thought which make it impossible for the symbols and observances in which Christianity has formerly expressed itself to seem valid or meaningful any longer, and that religion, from now on, must find itself a new wardrobe. Many who still retain a connection with the churches and attend their services feel this, but are convinced that they must give their loyalty to the older forms of religious expression until adequate newer ones are found to replace them. Others, however, including those who most influence church teaching and practice, feel differently and deplore the present agnosticism as a temporary aberration. The unfortunate effect of this is further to alienate those no longer within the church. Whereas formerly it was the place from which they guiltily stayed away, now it is the place to which they would not dream of going because it no longer seems to point the way to truth, and those within it cannot understand how others think.

The implications of this situation for education are that large numbers of children are being influenced by it both in their attitude and in their knowledge. Since parents now openly admit that they find the orthodox expression of Christianity irrelevant or unhelpful, children are less likely to have a receptive attitude to it. Further, their background knowledge of religious ideas and practices is likely to be small. For instance, a teacher in Coventry in 1964 asked a sixth form what denominations had churches in the city. They had no idea that churches differed and were divided into denominations. Nor were they interested to discuss this, for churches just did not enter into their list of things worth thinking about. If, therefore, the teacher of religion in schools is to do his work intelligently he must know something of the recent revolution in religious thinking and of how it has been caused. He must know how and why the majority of his pupils and their parents think as they do.

HOW THE SITUATION AROSE

Perhaps the most influential factor in present thinking is the 'scientific' attitude to reality. Before we can understand how this has caused us to modify our religious ideas we must consider the nature of religious thinking itself. Religion is fundamentally a man's attempt to explain to himself the meaning and purpose of his own existence. Yet since he is part of a much greater creation, he can discover purpose for himself only by reference to the purpose of the whole of creation. This leads him to postulate some explanation of how and why the universe came into being. For long periods of history men have been willing to accept without question the explanation that their civilisation has worked out, and usually this has involved belief in some kind of God. At times of unsettled thought individuals have felt it necessary to solve the conundrum afresh for themselves, and our time may be of such a kind. Until recently all such explanations have attempted to explain the created universe in terms of something other than itself—to work out a true *metaphysic*. This means that the statements of religion, apart from the religion called materialism, cannot be factual in the scientific sense. They must be in the form of metaphor, allegory, symbol, and imaginative parable. The symbols may be material things, and the allegories stories of material things, but they represent some truth that, without them, cannot be thought of at all. Further they are true only in so far as they are understood to be symbol and allegory. To take them literally is to distort them so that they represent falsehood rather than truth.

What symbols an age or civilisation chooses to explain its religious beliefs depend on its general intellectual assumptions. For instance, when it was believed that the earth was flat with a celestial region above and a dark subterranean one beneath it was possible to symbolise goodness as originating from a God above and evil as coming from a devil in hell beneath. Galileo and the discoveries of astronomy changed that. The basic intellectual assumption of our time seems to be that truth is to be discovered by the statistical investigation of the properties of the created universe, and our religion, to be meaningful, must be in terms acceptable to such an outlook. It is precisely here that we may have distorted and misunderstood the tenets of the Christian faith, by interpreting its symbols overliterally and evacuating them of meaning.

The Bible writers knew they were employing symbol and metaphor to convey otherwise inexpressible ideas, and would possibly have been amused to know how literally some of their more figurative pronouncements would be taken by later ages. They belonged to a time when thought was couched in terms of pictures and parables rather than abstract statements. Thus when the evangelists recorded Jesus' teaching of God as a heavenly father they knew that this described the relationship of God to humankind, and did not mean they believed he existed in an anthropomorphic form above the skies, even though for practical purposes of thinking they might find it necessary to imagine him as such. When St. John wrote in his epistle 'God is love, and he that dwelleth in love dwelleth in God, and God in him' (*I John* **4**, 16) he really meant what he said i.e. that it is through personal relationships that man comes into contact with the divine. The parable of the sheep and the goats in *Matthew* **25**, 31-46 conveys the same teaching.

Throughout the early days of the Church and during the Middle Ages a similar view prevailed. Living in small, closely-knit communities, men's main interest was in the interplay of human relationships. Their view of life was essentially dramatic. They saw it occasionally as a comedy, but usually as a stern tragedy in which good was fighting for survival against powerful and malignant ill, but it was the drama that engrossed their attention, not the stage or the properties which formed the *mise-en-scène*. It is significant in this connection that Tertullian in *Adversus Praxeam* chose to use in his description of the doctrine of the Trinity the word *persona*, an essentially dynamic word, meaning the role a person plays or the function he performs. Before the Reformation men saw God as an essential ingredient in the drama of life, with whom they could come into immediate contact through living, and not as an absentee creator standing in opposition to his creation but occasionally manifesting himself by physical modification of it.

In the past four hundred years attention has been transferred from the drama to the stage and the scenery. The careful investigation of the nature of matter and the discovery of the regular interaction of physical entities has changed the quality of human thinking as drastically as the application of those discoveries in technology has changed the manner of human life. The use of the scientific spirit and the success of the scientific method has had a threefold effect on religious thinking. Firstly, it has led to the assumption that the only reliable road to truth is the investigation of matter. Truth which can be demonstrated by reference to physical properties seems to us a superior and more reliable sort of truth. This modification of thought is clearly shown by the retreat of philosophy from metaphysics into logical positivism, which seems to be the verification of statements by reference to their physical demonstrability. The outcome is that ideas of spiritual entities have no esteem in modern thought. Secondly, the notion of the invariability of the law of cause and effect has become axiomatic. Everything that happens has, we think, a logical and explicable, and probably physical, cause.

This not only excludes the possibility of belief in miracle, but is also a matter of fact and undramatic view of the nature of reality, which at its most extreme subjects all human experience to the control of an impersonal destiny. It is in contrast to the dramatic view of the Middle Ages, and it is worth noting that the word 'dramatic' is now a term of disapprobation. Thirdly, it induces a literal-mindedness which either distrusts the use of symbolism and metaphor, or misunderstands it and mistakes the symbols and metaphors for a literal expression of truth. The latter fate has overtaken the figurative expression of Christian belief. Christians and non-Christians alike have come to regard its symbolic statements as expressions of scientific fact and its metaphors and parables as descriptions of historical events. Expounded in this way Christianity appears to be making statements which its early teachers would not have accepted and which are untenable by those affected by scientific thought.

The idea of God that emerged from this new type of human thinking was that he must be some kind of physical entity, who created the universe by some kind of physical energy, and stands outside it, watching it, and occasionally intruding into it, again in physical manner, to modify it in the form of a miracle. The fact that the miracles happened long ago seemed to lessen their conflict with scientific law, which had been discovered since, and the confining of scientific investigation to the surface of the earth meant that God could still be imagined as living somewhere out in space. Such a theological conception was not untenable to most people until well into the present century. More recent investigation upward into space and downward into the atom has undermined it. Such a God cannot be found, and if the word God is to mean anything at all he must be rediscovered in the depth of human experience and in the drama of human life. Furthermore religion can become meaningful again only if its symbolic statements are recognised as symbolic and its metaphors seen to be metaphorical.

The need to disentangle the truths of Christianity from over-literal thought and to recognise afresh the inward and spiritual nature of religion had begun to be recognised by the 1940s by certain theologians, chiefly Tillich in America and Bultmann and Bonhoeffer in Germany. Those who were not theologians were conscious of a conflict between the scientific view of the world which coloured their thoughts and Christianity as it was popularly expounded. This conflict affected their religious behaviour, but a guilty sense of infidelity prevented its being openly discussed. Many were troubled with religious doubt but did not talk about their problems. It was simpler to ignore religion. In 1963 J. A. T. Robinson, the Bishop of Woolwich, published his famous *Honest to God* which gave expression to similar doubts. The importance of this book was not that it stated anything of importance that had not previously been said by the theologians mentioned above, or that it provided a positive re-expression of Christian beliefs, but that it was written by a Bishop. If he could discuss religion in this way, then the ordinary man might do so as well, which was what he had been wanting to do for some time. *Honest to God*, wrote Roger Lloyd, a year after its publication, 'put theology on the map and caused it to be discussed in all sorts of places where the name of God was never more than a casual oath' (*The Ferment in the Church*, p. 29). Religion is no longer a fixed set of doctrines which those who find them acceptable think it benevolent to try and transmit, but an open search for truth and a matter of personal choice. This open approach to it radically affects the teaching situation.

IMPLICATIONS FOR RELIGIOUS TEACHING

Theologically the present time is an age of demolition not of reconstruction. We have 'a site but no house'. The symbols and modes of thought in which religion has been expressed since the Reformation have been shown to be either misleading or meaningless to a generation whose thought is regulated by the scientific temper. Yet no new and more acceptable symbols have been found to put in their place. Tillich has said that we must think of God as the 'ground of being' and not as a transcendant quasi-physical entity. 'The name of this infinite and inexhaustible depth and ground of all being is *God*. That depth is what the word *God* means. And if that word has not much meaning for you, translate it, and speak of the depths of your life, of the source of your being, of your ultimate concern, of what you take seriously without any reservations', (*The Shaking of the Foundations*, p. 63). One can see roughly what this means, but only roughly. The difficulty is one of imagination. Before this concept of 'depth of being' can become definable and teachable we have to find some way of imagining it. That is, we have to find some symbols by which we can imagine it, and so far the new theology has not produced these symbols. The Bishop of Woolwich in his later book *The New Reformation?* (1965) argues that the duty of religious people at present is to cease to think theologically altogether and to think anthropologically instead. 'Fundamentally I believe that we can and must accept a new starting point. In other words, we must recognise the fact that man's question is *in the first* instance a question about man and not about "God"—a word which is becoming increasingly problematic to our generation and which has to be "brought in" more and more unnaturally into any discussion' (p. 34). Further the volume of essays called *Soundings* (Ed. A. R. Vidler, C.U.P., 1962), which was an attempt by a number of academic and responsible theologians to assess the validity and significance of their study, and represents the scholarly counterpart of *Honest to God*, boldly admits that it is probably impossible for theology to make any positive meaningful statement in the twentieth century. The opening paragraph includes this sentence: 'We can best serve the cause of truth and of the Church by candidly confessing where our perplexities lie, and not by making claims which, so far as we can see, theologians, are not at present in a position to justify' (p. ix). The sum total of this is that the old theology has passed away but the new has not arrived. The old house is in ruins and we have no more than a vague notion of the shape of the building that may eventually replace it.

The teacher of religious instruction may feel that this places him in an impossible position, by removing from him the subject matter of his craft and leaving him with nothing to teach. Is he to continue with the old material and be content that it seems digestible to the few, or is he to try to convey the new but vague ideas to the older children and risk causing confusion rather than enlightenment, or is he justified in suspending operations until the community has made up its mind on theological matters and decided what it wants its children taught? The law and the agreed syllabuses require him to choose the first of these three possibilities, and some teachers of the subject are happy to accept this. Others, however, feel that this causes the subject as taught in schools to be quite out of touch with the situation that the children encounter outside school.

The search for new theological expression has not in fact taken his subject matter from the religious teacher, but it has removed it to the realm of profound, subtle, and mature thought. To work out what is meant by such expressions as 'the ground of being' and to form symbols which make it imaginable is a matter for experts, and not schoolchildren. The brighter sixth form minds may be able to discuss it with some degree of comprehension, but it is unlikely to have any impact on thirteen-year-olds in the C stream. The situation is in part analogous to that found in physics. To understand fully the nature of matter as described by leading scientific philosophy demands an understanding of the implications of the theory of relativity and of the theory of atomic structure. These difficult ideas can reasonably be introduced to pupils at the 'A' level stage and beyond. In the lower forms physics is still taught with a Newtonian background, and confines itself to ideas which are ultimately less accurate, but which are still of practical application within the realm of everyday experience. The teacher of religion may similarly feel that his subject can be discussed with reference to reality only by the brighter pupils in the year or so before they leave school. But there the analogy ends. For whereas the older physics can still be taught at the elementary stages with some practical application, the simpler forms of the older theology, apart from its moral application, are open to serious questioning. The problem for the teacher is what to teach to the younger children, who cannot discuss the abstruse new ideas of the modern search for religious meaning. In 1963 Sir Richard Acland argued that this problem does not exist (*We Teach Them Wrong*, pp. 42-4). He says that in growing up the child passes rapidly through all the mental stages that the human race has traversed in the course of evolution. The younger child has, he maintains, the mental outlook of several centuries ago and can find meaning in the theology of several centuries ago. Consequently no great changes are needed in the earlier stages of religious instruction. This theory may be questioned on two grounds. Firstly, while younger children may possibly have the mental capacity of an earlier stage of evolution, it is doubtful whether once they are out of the stage of extreme infancy they can have the mental outlook of former times. The presuppositions of adult thought, what the world around them accepts as real or rejects as unreal, quickly influence them and colour their outlook. Secondly, even if they accept some of the simpler tenets of the old-style religious thought where will such knowledge lead? Once it would have been preparing them to progress to more profound classical theological ideas. Now those ideas have passed. The new expression of theological ideas is so far sundered from the old that to train children in the early stages of the old is no way of preparing them to accept the more complex ideas of the new. Rather is it laying upon them the task at some stage of rethinking all that they have learned and translating it into different terms. There is evidence (which will be discussed more fully in Chapter 3) to suggest that being subjected to the older teaching at an early stage inhibits children from thinking maturely about religion at a later age. They do not embark upon the necessary rethinking and translating, but reject religion as childish and cease to think seriously about it at all. The problem therefore remains of what to teach in the lower parts of the school which will prepare the children to think in terms of the new theological concepts and encourage them to do so when they have the mental capacity and experience necessary for such thought.

Another problem for the religious teacher in an age of theological change is the relationship of his teaching to that given in the organised religious bodies, the churches. There is a built-in inertia about organised religion that makes it slow to reflect change in theological thought. Thus although many who are trying to think out a vital religious expression for a technological age are members of the Christian Church, they are a minority. Their thinking has up to the present had little effect on the weekly worship and teaching in the average church. Their writings are frequently held in suspicion by those who attend those churches, where their books are as often attacked as studied. The resistance to the new thought is particularly strong in the Church of England which is bound by law to use forms of worship which are in terms of the old symbols and thought-forms. Where, in this time of cleavage, between attempts at vital and realistic religious thinking on the one hand, and Christianity as it is taught and practised in the church along the road on the other, is the teacher in the county school to put his loyalty? The reserved teacher in the controlled school or the teacher in the aided school who is in sympathy with the more critical approach to religion may find this problem more acute.

How far the individual teacher feels this to be a problem depends on his own personal view. If he is one of the many who are still secure in the fold of the church and still finding its traditional expressions helpful, he will have little difficulty. He will be content to teach the Bible and Christian ideas which are within the syllabus as they have long been taught; he will hope that those who respond will attach themselves to some existing worshipping community; he will invoke the authority of the Church to support his teaching, while being hurt that such authority is not recognised by some of his pupils. But the teacher who joins with the majority of his fellow-countrymen and is critical of the older expression of religion is in a different position. He may not feel that his teaching has the authority of official Christianity and wish that it had, for fear that it may be a personal idiosyncracy. He may wonder whether he should subject his pupils to a possible conflict between what they hear at church and Sunday School and what they hear in the classroom. He may be at a loss to know how to guide the expression of religious ideas that his pupils acquire, if the local church does not make provision for this. He may fear complaints and opposition from children, parents and educational and ecclesiastical authorities who do not yet welcome the teaching of religion as a personal search for meaning. Such teachers—they are not numerous at present but they are growing—may find their consciences strained and perhaps something should be done to ease them if the teaching of religion in schools is to be influenced by the new theological thinking and revitalised by it.

3

How children think about religion

The most formative influence in education in the past thirty years has been the information provided by the psychologists of how children think, and of the age at which their ideas develop. This has given particular guidance as to the time when children are ready and able to advance into a new field of understanding. Since religious thought is not different in quality from other thought, but merely ordinary thought exercised on religious ideas, religious instruction should be open to this influence no less than other subjects. Moreover, a number of researches have been conducted into the way in which religious ideas are formed in the growing mind which are likely radically to influence the future strategy of religious education, and therefore no religious teacher can afford to be without knowledge of the general findings of these researches and their implications for teaching.

HARMS' THREEFOLD CLASSIFICATION

These researches have shown that children's religious ideas

do not increase in number and profundity only. They also change qualitatively, and pass through several definable stages. The exact age at which any particular child passes from one stage to the next depends upon his intelligence, motivation, and many other factors, but the phases of growth may be fairly accurately described. One of the earliest attempts to do this was that of Harms ('The Development of Religious Experience in Children', *American Journal of Sociology*, vol. 50, no. 2, 1944), who asked a large number of children in the U.S.A. to draw a picture of what they thought God looked like and to write comments about the nature of God on the back of the picture. In the case of children unable to write, the teachers recorded their spoken comments. The material was classified and from the classification Harms distinguished three stages of religious growth.

(*a*) *The fairy-tale stage*, usually found in children between the ages of 3 and 6 years, when both the pictures and comments suggest they make no distinction between religion and fairy tales, and accept each with similar credulity. God belongs to the realm of benevolent giants, and Bible miracles are confused with magic. A little thought can show how these ideas occur. At this stage children's experience of the world is small, and they have not learned how far the possible is limited. The imagination is therefore free to roam and the imaginable is identical with the real. They find it possible to accept any ideas put to them, whether religious or otherwise, without demur.

(*b*) *The realistic stage*, roughly corresponding to 7-12 years of age, when children's religious thoughts seem to be influenced by the fact that they are then learning rapidly about the nature of the material world. At this stage they are interested in things and events and inclined to be matter-of-fact. Their frequent question 'Is it true?' is really asking 'Does it exist (materially)?' or 'Did it happen (historically)?' The real for them is material and historical. Consequently they think of God as an an-thropomorphic figure having direct physical influence in the world.

(c) *The individualistic stage*, which is reached about the age of 12 years and continues through adolescence. Here Harms found a wide variety of interpretations of religion, but discerned among some of his subjects the personal and mystical approach to religion, which sees God not as a gigantic and picturable physical power, but as a spiritual being with whom it is possible to have a personal re-lationship.

It is noteworthy that while all children pass through the first two stages, not all of them advance into the third stage. Harms commented on the tempo of religious de-velopment which is much slower than development in other fields of experience, and it would seem that not all children complete the course of religious development. It may be that the pursuits of scientific and technological thought are impelling them to remain in the realistic stage, and that one of the tasks of religious education is to help them to progress into the individualistic stage when genuine religious thinking takes place.

Numerous other writers, among them Kupky (*The Religious Development of Adolescents*, Macmillan, N.Y., 1928) and Basil Yeaxlee (*Religion and the Growing Mind*, 1939) have commented on this threefold development and it would seem that, as a broad classification, it gives an accurate account of religious growth. A more detailed investigation by Ronald Goldman has given us a much sharper view of the processes involved. This research is already having a decisive effect on thinking about religious education, and anyone who embarks upon religious education is well advised to acquaint himself with it in detail. It is not within the scope of this book to give more than a cursory account of it, and readers are urged to study it fully in Dr. Goldman's *Religious Thinking from Childhood to Adolescence*, (1964).

THE GOLDMAN RESEARCH

Piaget, in his books *The Child's Conception of the World*, *The Child's Conception of Causality* (Routledge and Kegan Paul, 1929 and 1930, respectively) and *Logic and Psychology* (University of Manchester Press, 1953), had described the types of thinking possible for children at various ages. He distinguished three stages and it is worth noting that the ages occupied by each stage correspond closely to those used by Harms' threefold classification. The first stage (2-7 years) Piaget calls 'intuitive' or 'pre-operational' thinking. In it the child's thought is unsystematic and fragmented. He cannot relate one thought to another or draw a logical inference from a fact. When he tries to do so the transition is often illogical—hence the many strange remarks, which some find quaint or amusing, made by young children. The second stage is 'concrete operational thinking' (7-11 years) when the child is able to relate visible and tangible things and draw inferences from them, but cannot generalise or think verbally or abstractly. The final stage (12 years upwards) is that of 'formal operational thinking' when it is possible for the adolescent to reason hypothetically and deductively, and to understand symbolic and abstract terms.

Goldman started from Piaget's description of general thinking and undertook a careful and detailed research to discover whether children's thoughts about religious notions followed this pattern. He chose 200 schoolchildren from areas in the Midlands and Southern England, 20 in each year of age, representing a typical cross-section of those 'normally exposed to religious education under the requirements of the 1944 Education Act' and each of these he interviewed at length. During the interviews he told the subjects three Bible stories (Moses and the Burning Bush, the Crossing of the Red Sea and the Temptation of Jesus) and he showed them three pictures (a family entering a church, a child kneeling in prayer at a bedside, and a mutilated copy of the Bible). There followed a number of predetermined questions to discover the meaning that the story or the picture had for the child. Only statisticians can appreciate the detailed accuracy with which Dr. Goldman classified and analysed these responses, but the outcome of this meticulous work was that religious thinking follows the Piaget scheme and that 'religious thinking employs the same modes and methods as thinking applied to other fields' (*op. cit.* p. 66), and thus, he found, the more intellectually gifted children generally passed from one stage to another at an earlier age than their fellows. However, Goldman discerns intermediate stages between the three described by Piaget, and it may make for clarity if this is regarded as a fivefold classification, thus:

(*a*) *Intuitive religious thinking.* At this stage children infer one particular fact from another particular fact, jumping

39

mentally from one to another even when there is no logical connection. Their thinking is inconsistent and influenced by irrelevancies. The question 'Why was Moses afraid to look upon God' evoked such replies as, 'God had a funny face' and 'Moses was frightened by the funny face'. One child, when asked why the ground on which Moses stood was holy, replied, 'Because it had grass on it'. According to another, Jesus didn't turn stones into bread, although he was hungry, because 'The bad man wouldn't let him go. The bad man didn't say please'. This suggests that Bible stories told to very young children may be understood in all sorts of strange ways unintended by the teller and the way they are understood depends largely on what other ideas the child has had recently in mind.

(b) *Intermediate stage between intuitive and concrete religious thinking.* When the ability to think operationally begins to form, children seem to become aware of the limitations of their intuitive thoughts and try to produce logical explanations. Their first efforts, however, fail and so there seems to be an intermediary stage of unsuccessful concrete operational thinking. This is shown by the answer to the question of why Moses was afraid to look on God that 'God wears a beard and Moses didn't like beards'. This stage also produces circular arguments such as the reasoning that the ground on which Moses stood was holy because God had blessed it, and God had blessed it because it was holy. The inaccuracy of these early attempts at reasoning mean that Bible stories are still liable to complete misunderstanding.

(c) *Concrete operational religious thinking.* At this stage children can classify ideas, think systematically, and make reasoned conclusions within a restricted field. This 'operational' thinking is limited in two ways. Firstly it can function only when it is being exercised on visible and tangible objects—or in the case of a story, things which would be visible or tangible to the characters in the story; secondly it cannot go beyond the bounds of the child's own experience. This means that Bible stories are understood in a literal manner, and the events in them explained in terms of the simple everyday science that the child has acquired. Goldman found that children explained Moses' reluctance to approach the burning bush as fear of being burned or blinded. The Red Sea was thought to have been parted by God's hands. Jesus didn't turn stones into bread because he was hiding his magic from the devil. If he used it, he would reveal its presence and the devil would steal it. The symbolic and parabolic nature of Bible stories is likely at this stage to elude them entirely. They are incapable of making the spiritual interpretation that such material demands, and the use of this sort of story, far from giving the view of God and his relationship to the world that is desired, may be reinforcing a crudely anthropomorphic view which will prevent the development of a truer and more spiritual view at a later date. It is possible that many children do not progress beyond concrete operational thinking in religion, and, when they find this view inadequate to explain their experience, cease to consider the subject worthy of their attention.

(d) *Intermediate stage between concrete and abstract thinking.* Harms noticed that religious thought develops more slowly than thought in other fields. Goldman likewise notes that the transition from concrete to abstract operational thinking takes place in this subject at a later age than that suggested by Piaget, and comments that this may partly be due to the retarding effect, mentioned above, of the use in reading of Biblical material before children can understand its metaphorical nature. This slower development produces an intermediate period, between roughly the ages of 11 and 13 years, when there is an attempt at abstract thought about religion, but during which children find it difficult to shake off the older habits of concrete thought and so find themselves confused. As an illustration of this Goldman cites the child who tried to explain the bush burning 'without being consumed' by saying that the flame was 'some kind of holy, non-burning flame,' and the opinion that Jesus didn't turn stones into bread because he was 'trying to prove he could live without food'.

It is the opinion of the present writer that this intermediate stage is one of great importance for religious education. There is needed a strategy which will prevent children becoming hopelessly confused at this formative age, and enable them to pass easily and rapidly from concrete materialistic thinking about religion to a more abstract and spiritual view.

(e) *Abstract religious thinking*. After the age of 13 it becomes possible to think abstractly in terms of verbal propositions rather than actual situations. Hypothetical and deductive operations are undertaken, whereby the pupil starts from a theory and checks it by working back to the fact. Most important for our purpose, they can understand metaphor and realise that a story may be a means of conveying a truth rather than recounting an event. Thus in discussing the Bible narrative they are able to consider both what actually happened and what it signifies. Furthermore they are able to see in the story particularised examples of general fact. One answer to the question of why Moses feared to look on God was that he had the sense of sin which is found in all men. Some of Goldman's subjects regarded the Temptation as a parable, such as the one who said 'He had gone to the desert to sort his thoughts out, and God gave him this test. It was his own conscience to see if he would give in or go on'.

Not all of this age are able to achieve fully abstract thought about religious matter and some still show a desire to fit the supernatural within the framework of what they know of the natural. Comment will be made on this later in the chapter. But not until this stage can the intellectual factor in religion be adequately dealt with, or the Bible reveal its spiritualised meaning, and a religious education which does not lead the pupils to this way of thinking is inadequate and likely to give the pupils an erroneous idea of what religion is about.

Goldman traces in detail the development through these five stages of the concept of the Divine Being, of holiness, of God's care for men, of his method of working in the world, of Jesus, of the problem of suffering, of prayer, of the church and of the Bible. Since it will be necessary to discuss later the use of the Bible in school, it will be convenient to mention briefly at this point what he discovered about pupils' ideas of the literal truth and authority of the scriptures. As regards the authority of the Bible, there appear to be three stages of thought. To approximately 10½ years it is respected as true and as having claim on our attention either because it is a big book (this only at a very early age), or because it is printed, or because some adult, mother, teacher or the Vicar, has said it is true. It derives its authority for young children from some external person or circumstance. The next stage, which lasts for about two years, finds an intrinsic authority in the subject-matter it contains. For this age the Bible is true because it is about God or about Jesus. 'It must be true 'cause God and Jesus are in it.' This appears to be a general assumption and not a critical judgment. The critical appraisal of its authority does not occur until the third stage (12½ onwards) when the Scriptures are accepted as true because they are eyewitness accounts, or because they can be verified by reference to extra-Biblical sources (history, archeology, etc.) or because they are consistent with experience and so seem to have the ring of truth about them.

As regards the literal truth of the Bible. Goldman demonstrates that belief in this lingers until a comparatively advanced age. Until 13, some 80% of the children look on most of the Bible as literally true. In the next two years this drops to 57·5%. After the age of 15, the number of Goldman subjects who were literalists fell to 15%, but he points out that since these were young people who had stayed on at school and were presumably the more intelligent and highly educated, the percentage of the general population who remain literalists may be higher. The teacher who himself takes a literal view of the Bible may regard these figures as reasonably satisfactory, but others may wonder why literalism persists and whether uncritical views of the Bible, retained to an age when criticism is being encouraged in all other subjects, may not be giving a distorted view of religion and be the cause why many children reject it as childish at this stage.

RELIGIOUS PROBLEMS OF OLDER PUPILS

The aim of Goldman's research was to show chiefly by what stages children's religious thought develops to mature understanding. He was less concerned with the problems that arise once maturity is reached. However, he draws our attention to the tension felt by many adolescents between the theological view of the world, often a crude and literalist theological view, which they have acquired from their religious instruction, and the logico-scientific interpretation of existence that they acquire in other subjects. One result of this tension is their desire to interpret the supernatural in terms of the natural. For instance one attempt to explain the parting of the Red Sea was that God 'might take away the kinetic energy of the molecules on the surface area of the water and a sheet of ice would form to keep the water back'.

Further evidence of this tension, and the way in which sixth form grammar school pupils try to reduce it, is shown by an investigation which the writer directed for the Institute of Christian Education, (now called the Christian Education Movement) in which 2,278 pupils, about to take the 'A' level examination, were asked to express the intensity of their belief or disbelief in God and further to say what ideas of God they find acceptable and what unacceptable. Although these were the more intelligent and highly educated pupils it is possible that many others have similar difficulties in believing, even though they might express their difficulties less urgently and less elegantly.

There was no evidence of widespread disbelief; 23% of boys and 8% of girls were either atheists or inclined to be doubtful of God's existence. Roughly a quarter of each sex were undecided. That means about half the boys and well over two-thirds of the girls were favourably disposed to a theistic view. What is more important here is the concept they have in mind when they use the term God. Some describe God in traditional theological terms of

45

omniscient, omnipotent, merciful, loving Father, etc. A rather greater number say they believe there must be some power which began creation, which vaguely controls it and is possibly responsible for evolution and which gives purpose to life. The ingredients of their conception of this power emerge quite clearly. They regard it primarily as a remote, impersonal power, standing outside creation and in no way modifying it once the act of creation is completed. Physics, chemistry, and biology seem to them to be able satisfactorily to explain the tangible world as they immediately experience it. One wrote, 'I believe there must have been something which caused the beginning of the world, but I do not see that it can be classed as God since it seems to have no power over its own creation'. Secondly they feel the need to try and describe this power in words that were within scientific terms of reference and will be acceptable to their scientific conscience. They are inclined to refer to it as a 'driving force' or a 'starting force', which they envisage as a mechanical form of energy.

The comments included frequent complaints that there is no evidence to justify particular religious beliefs. Lack of evidence is not regarded as warranting suspended judgment or accepting an act of faith as a working hypothesis, but for disbelief until some cogent evidence is discovered. By evidence they appear to mean material phenomena, susceptible to one of the five senses, and it is often called 'concrete evidence'. All this seems to suggest that those whose thoughts are strongly conditioned by the scientific attitude are searching for some spiritual explanation of existence, but finding it elusive because it cannot be expressed within those mechanical terms which alone they find satisfying.

They appear to be searching for an assurance that life has point. A very small number find this in being part of the evolutionary chain or in social service, but most of them seem to be seeking support for their conviction that life should be a happy, enjoyable and purposive experience. This is shown by their sensitive reaction to the problem of evil (which seems to be a considerable obstacle to theistic belief), by their description of their acceptance of God as a benevolent, forgiving, not over-censorious controller of destiny, and their inclination to deny that such a being would pass adverse judgment on human actions. Whether this is the result or the cause of the demand for a more permissive morality is difficult to decide. They have a strong feeling, however, that religious instruction is at present of little help to them in their search. This is partly because they think, perhaps mistakenly, that it is offering them too unsophisticated a solution. The comment that God is not a being (i.e. a physical entity), that he is not an old man above the skies and that he didn't make the world in six days is unexpectedly common. The vehemence with which they make this repudiation suggests they think that such crude anthropomorphisms are what Christianity has to offer as an explanation of experience. The other reason for their suspicion of religious instruction is the respectable conviction that, since each person's belief can be genuine only if based on his own experience and no one else's, they must work out a faith for themselves. They are sure that no ready-made scheme of belief can help them, and show ready scorn for any who try to present them with such. One boy writes, 'Before I commit myself to any belief I must be sure that I can understand it. I must question everything before a decision.' And another says, 'There should be discussion rather than being told what is right by someone . . . who alleges that he himself and his doctrines are infallible'.

THE EFFECT OF ATTITUDE ON RELIGIOUS LEARNING

In an article in *Educational Review* of June 1958, entitled 'The Problem of Communication in Religious Education', Yeaxlee reported the opinion of experienced teachers that pupils with an indifferent or hostile attitude to religion were less able to absorb the subject matter of religious instruction than those favourably disposed. This led K. E. Hyde to undertake an investigation into the exact effect of attitudes on religious learning. He constructed five carefully validated tests, one of attitude to religion, one of religious behaviour, two of religious concepts, and one of attainment based on a specific teaching syllabus. These were administered to 1,977 pupils in four schools, where the religious education was seriously undertaken by specialist teachers. A full account of the tests and of the relation of their findings may be read in Hyde's *Religious Learning in Adolescence* (1965), but mention must be made here of its more significant general conclusions. Among his findings three things stand out.

1.   There is a connection between religious behaviour and a favourable attitude to religion. Children from church-going homes and with specific connections with a religious organisation are much more favourably disposed to religious ideas and the 'facts' of the scripture lesson than are the others.

     It was found that children's attitude scores were very strongly related to their professed religious behaviour. (p. 41)

Attitudes more favourable to religion always seem to be associated with the church-going children, whose attitude score remained remarkably consistent over the whole age range investigated. (p. 32)

Hyde's research was not designed to show whether the attitude caused the church-going or the church-going caused the attitude. Possibly the two go together and are so closely interlinked that it would be almost impossible to trace any causal link between them.

2. Those with favourable attitudes tend to learn and to retain religious concepts more easily than the pupils with unfavourable attitudes.

Their attitudes were found to have considerable influence upon their conceptual development. Children with higher attitude scores showed greater conceptual insight than children with lower attitude scores. Continued religious learning through the secondary school age range was related to higher attitude scores. . . . Without this positive religious attitude, expressed in activities of church-going and prayer, conceptual development does not take place. (p. 4)

3. Whereas children with favourable religious attitudes retain them throughout their school life and continue to learn, those with weak or unfavourable attitudes tend to become more opposed to religious ideas and to learn less and less. With these children the task of the religious teacher becomes increasingly difficult.

Church-going is associated with more positive religious attitudes and without this experience of religious involvement religious attitudes become less positive as children pass through adolescence. . . . The children who did not attend church (and in the present sample there was a tendency for church-going to fall off in the older age groups) showed a regular decline in religious attitude scores over the whole age range tested. (pp. 32-3)

This decline in favourable attitude can turn from a negative disinclination to learn to a positive rejection of religious ideas and an open hostility to them.

It must be noted that the age at which marked deterioration of attitude is observed, coincides with the period of mental development when critical thinking emerges. So it comes about that critical power may be emotionally orientated against religious belief while the assertions of a popular humanism, with its mechanical explanation of life and its rejection of the spiritual is uncritically accepted. Thus a prejudice against religion becomes firmly established while religious ideas remain confused and inadequate. (p. 92)

IMPLICATIONS FOR RELIGIOUS EDUCATION

It may help for clarity if the four implications of these researches for religious education are enumerated at this point, although they will later be discussed more fully.

Firstly, there is the overriding importance of training attitudes, without which learning takes place hardly or not at all. This involves the question of how attitudes are formed, and what can be done in school to inculcate or modify them. It may be that social and home influence, reaching far back into pre-school life and infancy, are decisive in attitude formation and that the teacher can do little but accept the attitudes that the children bring with them and work within their limitations.

Secondly, Goldman's findings have shown the need to select Bible material which conveys its true meaning to the children at the age at which they hear it. Bible stories which convey truth in a symbolic form and need abstract thought for full understanding may, if used at too early an age, convey ideas different from what their teacher intends. True, when questioned, the pupils may appear to give satisfactory answers, but there is evidence that they are repeating memorised words to please teacher without understanding their meaning. For instance, Goldman tells of the child who said, 'Man cannot live by bread alone', when asked why Jesus did not turn stones into bread, but when asked, 'Why cannot man live by bread alone?' answered, 'Because he needs butter and jam to go on it' (*Religious Thinking in Childhood and Adolescence*, p. 167). Use of abstract material at an immature age may give the wrong impression of what religion is about and cause the pupil to reject it, before he is able to think abstractly and deeply about it. There is need for much more investigation of how children understand Biblical material, a careful grading of it, and a construction of syllabuses which introduce the right stories at the right time.

Thirdly, however careful their previous education both in content and presentation, there is a period of transition at the age when children begin to think abstractly. They begin to be capable of understanding their previous religious learning at greater depth, and they need to be helped systematically to rethink their religious ideas at this stage. Unless this is done there arises a conflict between what they have been taught about the nature of the world in the religious instruction lesson and what they are told in their scientific studies. If they can be shown that the religious view and the scientific view of reality are not two alternative and mutually exclusive explanations, but two different ways of looking at the same thing, each valid and useful in its proper context, they are not likely to reject religious thoughts for good.

Fourthly, in the later years at school, free but informed and guided discussion is needed, so that the pupils can work out for themselves what their personal religious beliefs are. Doctrinal ideas which are based on other people's experience, or the wisdom of the past, or which have to be accepted on the authority of the teacher or a church, will have little chance of a hearing except with those of convinced Christian background who have already accepted the doctrine anyway. But a sharing of experience by both pupils and teacher and an attempt to discover its religious implications, albeit pedagogically more difficult and academically less systematic and satisfying, may meet with more general success. At this stage teachers would be advised to 'help their pupils towards critical choice, and to see the aim of religious education in terms of personal search rather than the imparting of a body of fact' (R. Acland *et al*; *An Open Letter to L.E.A. Religious Advisory Committees*, 1965).

4

Aims in religious education

Before it is possible to outline a programme of practical
religious instruction which takes into account the new
theological ideas and the fresh understanding of the development of religious concepts, which have been outlined in
previous chapters, it is necessary to consider what aims the
religious teacher can reasonably set himself. What exactly
is he trying to do?

These aims must seem adequate to the teacher, worth-
while to the children, and useful to the community. There
was perhaps a time when any knowledge was considered
a useful acquisition, which gave the possessor a personal
satisfaction and evoked the admiration of those who did
not share it. But with general education and so much to be
known, a selection has to be made of what is to be taught,
and the test is the contribution that the subject will make
to a pupil's personality or his usefulness as a workman or
citizen. The decline in the study of the classics is perhaps
an example of the application of this criterion, as, in the
opposite way, is the fashionable demand for more technology in the higher forms of education. Some subjects

succeed in getting taught when their utility has declined. because they are a traditional part of education and no one has questioned their usefulness. Is religious education of such a sort? Can it be shown to be making a contribution to the pupil's growth, either as an individual or as a citizen, or is it so much intellectual lumber? There is all the more need to answer this question at a time when many would regard theological knowledge as lumber of a very old-fashioned kind.

Several aims are postulated for the subject, which must be discussed and evaluated.

TO TEACH THE BIBLE?

Religious instruction in this country must consist largely, if not entirely, of instruction in Christianity, because that has been the predominant religion in this part of the world and has been interwoven with our culture. Therefore, a study of the book which Christianity regards as sacred must be included at some stage, and to teach about the contents of the Bible must be one of the aims of the religious teacher. But how important an aim is it? Is it so important as to be the only aim, or is it a subsidiary aim, useful in so far as it leads to the achievement of a profounder purpose? Are those teachers who conscientiously impart the facts of Hebrew history and its background and the narrative details of the Gospels and the Acts, teaching religion as well as ancient history and literature?

The claim that teaching a class Bible facts is an adequate educational aim is usually based on one of two theories. The first is the belief that knowledge of the Bible will in an undefined and mystic way have a beneficial effect on the pupil and produce in him faith and moral character.

The most extreme adherents to this view would maintain that this benefit is imparted to the reader irrespective of the manner in which he understands what he is reading. The Bible, they say, is 'inspired' in such a way as to give it this unique influence which is shared by no other literature. Teachers who hold this belief about the nature of Biblical inspiration will regard the imparting of Bible facts as an adequate aim in itself. Others may wonder whether this is not ignoring the information about the nature and origin of the Biblical material that historical and critical scholarship has discovered, and whether it is possible for the more primitive parts of Hebrew history and such writings as *Psalm 58* to have such a civilising effect upon the reader.

The second justification advanced for Bible study as an end in itself is its cultural and literary value. Its thought-forms have influenced our ways of thinking, its metaphors have been adopted into our manner of speech, and it has influenced much of our literature both in idea and expression. Because of this, and because of its intrinsic literary worth, knowledge of the Bible should be part of the equipment of a moderately educated man. How far is this justification valid? The influence of the Bible in thought and speech would appear to have decreased. The older parliamentary speeches made not infrequent references to it, and the characters in the works of Thomas Hardy used its words in common conversation. A Biblical quotation today, apart from the Golden Rule and such a hackneyed phrase as 'turning the other cheek' will pass unidentified. Now that the Bible is little read by most people outside school, its effect on general thought and language is lessening and so undermining the cultural argument for studying it inside school. It is true, however, that its influence is great on much standard literature, and that full appreciation of this demands knowledge of the Bible text. For instance, Shakespeare appears to have been influenced by the closing chapters of *I Samuel* when writing *Macbeth* (compare Act I scene III with chapter **23**) and the final scenes of *Julius Caesar* (compare Act V scene III with chapter **31**), and Bottom the Weaver appears to parody a writing of St. Paul (see *Corinthians* **2**, 9 and *A Midsummer Night's Dream*, Act VI scene I). But though recognition of this may deepen our appreciation of such literature, does it justify making Bible study the main aim of religious education?

It would seem, therefore, that although Bible study will be a part of religious education, it is insufficient by itself as an aim, except for those teachers who have a particular view of Biblical inspiration, and that we must look for some further aim for the subject.

TO TEACH MORALS?

One way in which religious instruction can justify itself on a utilitarian criterion is to claim that it gives practical guidance on behaviour and induces moral conduct. Conversations with parents about this subject rarely proceed far without some such remark as, 'Well, they ought to be taught the difference between right and wrong'. Though Christian doctrine and its mythology are no longer respected as they formerly were, yet Christian morality is still valued as a practical basis of conduct. Parents generally seem content that their children should be taught the doctrine and mythology, and then be allowed to forget it, provided that in the process they acquire some of the morality and practise it. None of the prefaces to the agreed syllabus explicitly state that moral teaching is the principle end of religious education, although the *City of Birmingham Agreed Syllabus of Religious Instruction* (1950) comes near to doing so when it states that the teaching should 'impress on the minds of the young enlightened Christian standards of individual and social responsibility' (p. 5) and when it says, 'Pupils should be made to realise that no other standards, such as those based on the rules of the game, can give so satisfactory and complete a solution to their problems, as those based on the mission and message of Jesus' (p. 24).

Naturally it is to be hoped that any religious teaching given to pupils will be sufficiently sincerely held as to be lived out in practice, and therefore moral teaching must be one of the aims of the religious teacher. We have to ask, however, is he to regard moral training as his chief purpose, or as a by-product? Most important, is it possible to give moral teaching without involving some more ultimate objective, such as the imparting of philosophical theories or religious beliefs? Teaching moral conduct demands three processes: (*a*) telling the pupils under what circumstances an action is right and under what circumstances it is wrong; (*b*) explaining to them why this distinction is made between the two types of conduct and convincing them that it is a valid one; (*c*) persuading them to choose the right conduct and abstain from the wrong. In an age of settled moral convictions, the first of these three processes would be a matter of teaching fact, presenting no more educational problems than the teaching of any other fact; this is probably still so in dealing with younger children, where sophisticated moral problems do not arise, and the pupils are not yet capable of abstract theorising but are prepared to accept authoritative distinction of what is right and what is wrong. With older classes, however, the second process assumes the greater importance. Not only are they capable of moral choice, but also, the widespread disagreement in the community as to what is right conduct, requires them to do so with little clear guidance. A time when moral standards are uncertain allows a good deal of experimental conduct under the term 'permissive morality'. This may not greatly affect older persons who have formed a habitual pattern of behaviour, but it faces adolescents with the responsibility of perpetual moral choice and of working out the rightness and wrongness of each action from first principles. This may be no bad thing, and some would argue that this is true morality, but it lays on the teacher the responsibility of helping his pupils discover what the first principles are. It involves discussing with them such questions as, 'What is life?', 'What is it for?', 'What are people?', 'How far am I justified in ignoring others and pleasing myself?', 'Is it right to inflict pain?', etc. To discuss these questions something very much like religion has to be invoked and their full consideration would include taking cognisance of what the great world religions have said about them. It is difficult, therefore, to achieve the second of the three parts of moral instruction without departing from the field of ethics into that of religion, unless the foundation of moral action is to be found in some social theory such as the good of the community or the well-being of the state.

There remains, however, the third process which is helping the pupils to act morally when they are able to decide what actions are right for them. Here the question arises of whether a naturalistic theory of morals will provide sufficient motivation? History has a number of examples of attempts to define moral action as that which is conducive to the welfare of the state, but these have generally found it necessary to support themselves by a system of strong sanctions and police enforcement. The social hedonist ethic of 'the greater good of the greater number' has an appeal only to the highly intellectual and easily breaks down when it conflicts with personal advantage, provided the individual feels he has a reasonable chance of getting away with his deviation. The failure of the repeated government appeals in Britain in recent years for wage restraint and moderation of prices in the interest of the country's economy is an example of this. The good of the community is an effective spur to moral action only if it is supported by an almost mystical view of the community, or the realisation that in the community the individual personality reaches its highest development. But development of the individual involves the question of the nature of man, and we are back again in the realm of religion. It would seem that the true motivation to moral conduct is the realisation that this particular action is right because in some way it accords with the underlying purpose of creation, vague though our conception of that may be.

The foregoing suggests that it is difficult to separate moral education and religious education. Moral theorising and moral motivation both involve a subsistence of religious ideas. That is not to say that any one existing religion is the only basis for constructing a coherent moral system. Nor is it to argue that children should be persuaded to accept a set of tenets, which their elders question, in order to make them good. Still less is it suggesting that anyone should delude himself into subscribing to a creed which he does not genuinely believe because of the beneficial effect it will have on his conduct and the guidance it will afford him in making moral choice. A pretended belief will fail to perform such a function under the stress of genuine moral decision. But it does mean that a person, trying to decide what conduct is right for him, must have a sincere religious sensitivity. It will be argued later in this chapter that the cultivation of such a sensitivity is the prime aim of religious education. If the teacher makes moral training his first objective, and regards religious ideas as a means of attaining it, he may find he has succeeded in teaching a shallow belief which will not have the influence intended. On the other hand, if he leads his pupils to think sincerely and sensitively about the real religious problems of exist-ence he may find that he has also given help in moral problems.

Perhaps it is worth noting that children do not on the whole regard moral training as the purpose of religious instruction. When sixth formers were asked to state whether compulsory religious instruction should be given or not, and to state the reasons for their choice, of those who wished it to continue only 10·4% of boys and 4·3% of girls justified their views by saying that such instruction was needed for moral guidance. Most of them seemed to feel that the subject could and should offer more than that. The girl would not find undisputed support who wrote, 'Everyone is good after being taught it, and goes to heaven'.

TO CONVERT TO CHRISTIANITY?

In thinking of the aims of religious education it must be remembered that there are two levels at which the teacher may approach his task. He may either see his work as teaching facts about religion in general and about the details of particular creeds, or as helping pupils to adopt for themselves a religious view of life. There would be general agreement about the permissibility of the first attitude, but is the teacher who attempts the second going beyond his commission? The teacher of literature tries not only to give children knowledge of what has been written but also to induce appreciation of it. The science teacher hopes his classes will acquire both knowledge of facts and a spirit of scientific enquiry and a devotion to empirical accuracy. The teacher of religion can claim some justification for thinking he has more to do than teach facts. But there is a distinction between aiming to induce a religious attitude to life, and converting to any especial creed or denomination.

The idea that the purpose of religious education in schools is intended to convert children to the Christian faith is widespread. The churches reveal that they see it this way in the frequent demands that only those who are committed Christians should take part in it, and the occasional grumbling at its failure to produce instructed church-goers. Many teachers openly admit that they attempt to attach their pupils to some worshipping community. The older books on the subject specified discipleship as the final objective. For instance, Arundale in *Religious Education in the Senior School* (Nelson, 1944) says the teacher must ask himself, 'Am I turning out pupils merely packed with facts and dogma, or pupils who have a lively desire to "confess the faith of Christ crucified". . . ?' (p. 9). In *The Teaching of Religion* (Longmans, 1938), Braley states 'The teachers' supreme duty is to enable their scholars to know and love the Person, Jesus Christ' (p. 35). The *County Borough of Sunderland Syllabus of Religious Instruction* (1944) p. 13, maintains that 'the goal will be a life of worship and service in the Christian community'.

How far is such an aim proper? The existence of the agreed syllabuses presupposes that the teacher will not seek to advance the claims for allegiance to any particular denomination, but is it permitted to press the children to accept Christianity, provided they are allowed freely to choose between its different organised forms? In considering this there are three points to be borne in mind.

Firstly, the teacher has a function different from that of the evangelist or preacher. The latter holds certain beliefs which he thinks of supreme importance and which he tries to persuade others to share. His method is a vigorous, and sometimes vehement, assertion of those beliefs whereby he hopes to persuade his hearers of their urgency so that they too will become emotionally attached to them. He tries to dominate by enthusiasm and personality. No harm in that, provided everyone knows what is happening and the listeners can repudiate the ideas if they seem inaccurate and remove themselves from the evangelist's influence if they so wish. The teacher, however, though he may be an evangelist outside the classroom, has to work at less high pressure within it. He has a legal and psychological authority, especially with younger children, which the evangelist does not have, and which gives his ideas greater acceptability than they inherently possess. Further, the children cannot remove themselves from his influence. If he were to abuse this privileged position to propagate his political ideas there would be instant protest. Similarly in religion, the teacher may feel it *ultra vires* to transmit his own religious views, but think that his province is to help the pupils work out their own views on the basis of their experience. This will not prevent him explaining his own beliefs, and if he is confident of them he may reasonably hope that some of his pupils will be led by experience to accept them also; but it will prevent him from having conversion to Christianity as his chief aim and from pressing for a positive decision in the manner that is permitted to a preacher.

Secondly, to look on religious education as aiming at conversion—or, to use an emotionally less respectable term, indoctrination—is to put it out of line with present educational theory. There was a time when education was regarded as the teacher's imparting facts which were accepted on his authority and which children learned without understanding or being able to apply with the flexibility that comes from insight into their meaning. This worked well enough with those of good memory and docile temperament. But more recent practice shows that deeper and wider learning takes place if children are given the necessary experiences and then encouraged to find out things for themselves. For example, in early mathematics methods such as that of Cuisenaire have superseded authoritative demonstration of 'this is how to do sums'. Education has become a matter of investigation rather than indoctrination. To regard religious education as aiming at conversion is to prevent its being influenced by this educational advance, and to base it on ecclesiastical rather than educational principles. It may possibly be argued that the subject cannot be treated in the same way as others, since the ideas it attempts to convey are not susceptible to the empirical verification that is available in physics and mathematics. Religion, it is said, is not a matter that children can comprehend by investigation. It needs wider experience than they can bring to it and involves problems which even adults can answer only by recourse to revealed authority or faith. Yet children need some guidance in religion and must be given authoritative guidance in it just as they are given authoritative guidance on going to the dentist, or how to behave at table. One suspects that there is a confusion of thought here between ideas and actions. The statement that children need guidance in religion is an indirect way of saying that the virtue of religion is its good effect on conduct and that children should be directed to behave in a Christian manner. But while it may be permissible to give guidance on how to behave to children who have not yet the experience and insight to appreciate the implications of their actions, is it educationally sound, or even possible, to tell them what they are to think or believe? Is not this to give them adult ideas, which they cannot assimilate, but will hold as verbalisms to be repeated at appropriate occasions without being understood? It would seem more realistic to regard training in religious ideas as educationally similar to those of other subjects, basing them on the children's interpretation of experience, thus making them more genuine if less extensive.

The third objection to regarding the aim of religious education as conversion to Christianity is that at present it is achievable only to a limited extent. Indeed, if pursued too rigorously, it can be self-defeating. One of the arguments advanced for general religious instruction in schools is that if children do not hear of Christianity in the classroom they will not encounter it elsewhere. Yet they have every opportunity of meeting it, if they wish to do so, through Christian literature, broadcasts, and the weekly teaching of the local churches. If the number who avail themselves of these facilities is limited it is because of a widespread feeling that, at the present stage of human intellectual development, religion is an open question, and a minority find the Christian answers, in their traditional form, unable to close it. Though this does not greatly affect the younger children, adolescents are aware of this, albeit often unconsciously. They want the same freedom to choose or reject religious ideas that adults generally claim. They resent, therefore, what seems to them an unfair attempt to condition their opinions by an urgent pressing of Christian claims without examination of other possible views. From this springs their requests to study other world religions, which is not entirely based on the feeling that the grass is greener on the other side of the hedge, but rather from a feeling that they want to examine all the facts before making up their minds. The teacher who places conversion to Christianity before objectivity is likely to arouse a resentment which frustrates his efforts. Children write forcibly on this topic if allowed to do so. These are comments the writer has collected from various sources: 'I think you are more likely not to believe if it is forced upon you'. 'Scripture should be taught in an objective and unbiased way.' 'The teacher should not ride rough-shod over all criticism only to force his narrow and one-sided views.'

The suggestion that their lessons should not aim at conversion may, at first sight, be unacceptable to many teachers who undertake religious instructions, who are recruited mainly from members of the Christian church. Christianity is by its very nature a missionary faith and its keener adherents may feel infidelity if they do not avail themselves of every opportunity to obey the final injunction of St. Matthew's Gospel to 'Go, teach, and baptise' (**29**, 19). Moreover, if a teacher has found his religion brings him peace and purpose he will wish his pupils to acquire similar stability on the altruistic and educationally sound motive that it is for their own benefit and personal development. The desire to convert is not always ecclesiastical empire-building. Yet the Christian teacher can be assured that a non-evangelistic approach need not offend his conscience. If he is convinced of the truth of his religion, and that a thorough and sincere examination of human experience will lead to the decision that the Christian explanation of life is the most comprehensive and satisfactory, then he will be content to direct his pupils to that thorough and sincere examination, confident that by so doing he is advancing the Christian cause without the unfairness of hiding from his pupils that other ways of synthesising experience exist. To look on his work as pre-evangelisation rather than evangelisation may bring him slower and less obvious results, but it is educationally sounder and may, even from the Christian point of view, have more permanent effect.

TO HELP PUPILS HAVE A RELIGIOUS VIEW OF LIFE AND TO MAKE UP THEIR OWN MINDS ON RELIGIOUS QUESTIONS?

There is a growing feeling that religious education ought to be, in the jargon of today, 'open-ended'. This means it should have as its aim the giving to children of a religious view of life and then allowing them freely to make up their minds how that view shall express itself both in belief and practice. By 'religious view of life' is meant these attitudes: that man is one part of the whole complex of creation, the most highly developed and sensitive part, but none the less bound in a close relationship with the other parts which are to be respected and not ruthlessly exploited for the pleasure either of the individual or the species; that the individual has to live among his fellows, who have to be accorded the same consideration that he gives himself; that the whole has some overall purpose which has to be sought, even if it can only be partially understood; that apprehension of that purpose will give a clue to practical decisions and lead to the adoption of a moral code; and that aesthetic experience, as well as rational thought, can give awareness of that purpose, so that natural beauty and the arts are to be revered and cultivated as one of the roads to truth. It will be pointed out that this is the aim of education in general. What then is the specific aim of religious education? It will be to help cultivate these attitudes and, in particular, to help children to appreciate the questions that such attitudes raise, and consciously to seek the answers for themselves. These questions are of the type: 'Is creation adequately explained as a series of connected and mechanically caused events?'; 'Is there some spiritual reality of which the created world is but an outward manifestation?'; 'If so, does that spiritual reality reside in some single personal source which men have called "God"?'; 'Has an individual's life significance in its own right, or is it important only as part of some greater process?'; 'Is it possible for us to have any knowledge of what that significance is?'.

The aim of religious education would seem to be to help the children see, towards the end of their school life, when they are able to think sufficiently deeply, that these are the sort of questions that serious men have at times to ask and also to give them the information on which the answers may be based and then to encourage them sincerely to make up their minds for themselves. It is doubtful whether it is possible at present, even if it were desirable, to tell them the answers, since there is no agreement among adults as to what the answers are. Certainly it is wrong, and useless, to try to give them answers which the adult world does not generally accept, or finds still questionable. In a world in which religion is an 'open-ended' matter, religious education must also be 'open-ended'.

Giving the pupils the information from which they may find their own answer to ultimate questions will, however, include telling them what answers have been given to these questions in the past, and often found satisfactory over comparatively long periods. In Europe those answers have been the Christian ones. 'Open-ended' religious education will, therefore, largely involve teaching of the sources and faith of Christianity. It will include also some consideration of the ultimate explanations of existence given by other world religions, and of philosophies, such as Humanism and Marxism, which have maintained that adequate explanations can be framed without reference to the supernatural. But Christianity has contributed more than any other source to Western thought on these questions, and its historical importance would seem to justify making its study a major part of religious education.

Giving information about religion and encouraging his pupils to use it in making up their own minds about religious questions does not preclude the teacher from stating clearly his own views. Not to do so suggests either that he doesn't think any answers are possible, or that he doesn't think them worth seeking, and so encourages the children to dismiss religious questions as irrelevant. If he has deep convictions then they are part of the information he has to give, and he may reasonably tell his class that he believes that, if they think deeply, they will come to similar conclusions. This still leaves them free to accept other views. But if he gives the impression that he thinks his views are the only ones tenable by a thinking person, or if he insists that his pupils must share them and tries to argue into conformity anyone who has other ideas, then his lesson has ceased to be open-ended, and become doctrinal. If open-ended religious education involves a free expression of pupils' opinions, it also gives the teacher the right to express his opinions freely, provided he does so tactfully and with tolerance.

Such an aim as is here being discussed can be attempted only in the higher forms of the secondary school. Younger children do not frequently ask philosophical questions and, if they do, have not the maturity or mental equipment to attempt an answer. The question therefore arises again of what form religious education should take in the junior school. Should it be omitted and introduced only when the children can think religiously at full depth? The difficulty of this is that the pupils will not be able to think seriously about religious problems in adolescence unless they have had some earlier training in religion and been led progressively to the stage when they can make informed decisions about it. Not to have told them about religion before may inhibit their freedom of thought as surely as giving them intense dogmatic teaching, and would be comparable to expecting them to understand the calculus without first acquainting them with the more elementary forms of mathematics. Truly open-ended religious education can be achieved only if, in the preceding stages, children have been introduced to religious ideas which are relevant to them at each stage of their development, and which have been neither so vague as to make them feel that no answers are possible to religious problems, nor so dogmatic as to stifle freedom of thought. Moreover, it must be such as will be capable of expansion and development as their minds grow and their experience increases, so that they do not reject religious thoughts as childish just at the time when they begin to be able to make serious use of it.

It may not be possible to have one aim for all the stages of religious education. The impression is often given that teachers expect all the children to be entirely religious all the time. A more pragmatic approach might aim at making them capable of intelligent religious response by the time they leave school and of expecting of them something less at the intermediate stages. A series of phases by which the main aim may be finally achieved is discussed in the last chapter of this book.

5

The Bible in religious education

From the reformation to the twentieth century religion in Britain was mainly a Protestant Christianity which was Bible-based. The Scriptures were widely known and regarded as the source of Christian ideas and inspiration. Most of the time spent on religious instruction was assigned to learning of the contents or to committing to memory the words of the Bible. Even in the present century the agreed syllabuses generally prescribe examination of the Scriptures as the normal approach to religious education, and many teachers and pupils appear to equate religious instruction with Bible study. This is reflected in the tendency still to refer to the subject as 'Scripture'. The question arises, however, whether the Bible ought to be used as the starting point of religious education when it is no longer read and respected as it formerly was. Is present practice either educationally sound or likely to give an accurate knowledge of what the Bible itself says? Should the Bible play a different role in religious education in a non-Bible reading community from that which it plays when its words and concepts are contributing more directly to common speech and thought?

There is a growing demand that religious education cease to be 'Bible-centred' and become 'child-centred'. This springs from a recognition that Bible teaching alone is not adequate training in religious thought, that children find the words and the concepts of the Scriptures difficult to understand, that Bible stories often convey to pupils a meaning different from that intended both by the writer and the teachers, that Bible incidents seem to come from an age so different from ours that the teaching of the stories appears to have no relevance to the life we have to lead, and that attempts to make it relevant by appending to the lesson some forced modern moral or saying brightly, 'Now children, what do you think this means for us?' are inadequate. It is suggested, therefore, that instead of starting with the Bible and working to the children's experience, the teaching should start with experience, help the children to understand it, and then refer to the Bible to show how its stories can illuminate it and give guidance in understanding it. This leads to a less systematic study of the Bible and demands more thought and imagination on the part of the teacher, but it is in line with the educational practice of working from experience to understanding. The 'Readiness for Religion' series of work cards produced under the editorship of Dr. Goldman is an attempt to produce a practical teaching programme along these lines.

The issue, however, is more than a clear-cut dichotomy between Bible-centred and child-centred teaching. Full understanding of the place that the Bible can play in present education involves consideration of the manner in which the Bible has influenced Christian thought in the past, the nature of the Bible material itself, and the manner in which children of different ages understand that material.

THE INFLUENCE OF THE BIBLE ON CHRISTIAN THOUGHT

The influence of the Bible on the thoughts of Christians as a whole is different from its influence on the theological ideas of scholars. It is with the former that we are concerned here.

One of the assumptions of post-Reformation Christianity is that the Bible is the source of all Christian beliefs, every one of which can be traced back to an explicit scriptural statement. Therefore Bible reading and reasonable deduction from it will produce the instructed Christian. An examination of this assumption suggests that it misunderstands the historical significance of the Bible and the subtlety of its contribution to Christian ideas. The Church with its doctrines existed before the later parts of the Bible were written. The doctrines were being developed as Christians were led by their experience to realise the implications of their new faith. The reason for collecting certain books and canonising them was that there might be some record of the origin of the Christian Church and its early beliefs and practices, against which later developments might be checked, so that corruptions, which were not logical developments of the original faith, should not arise. While it has never accepted as Christian any beliefs which conflicted with a Biblical statement, the Church has not hesitated to propound doctrines which, although consonant with Bible teaching, go beyond it and develop and apply it. This has been done with a good conscience in the belief that the Holy Spirit would 'guide it into all truth' (*John* **16**, 13).

In practice this means that Christians as a body have worked out their faith in the light of experience and then referred to the Bible to check that they have interpreted that experience in a manner that accords with the original Christian tradition. Having decided what is the Christian attitude to a modern problem, they search the Scriptures to find a text which seems to relate to the matter in question to be certain that their ideas do not contradict those found in the Bible. This is justifiable and salutary, so long as it is realised what is being done. But an over-enthusiastic or unthinking use of this process may be detrimental in religious education, because it expects the pupils to read into Bible statements more than the plain words seem to some of them to warrant. For instance, one has heard teachers give vehement and detailed instruction of 'What Christ said about sex', whereas in fact the Gospels make few explicit references to that subject. What was being taught was wise and Christian, and might well have been said by Jesus were he to speak in our present situation, but to expect senior pupils to accept, on the authority of the Bible, teaching which the Bible does not seem to them to contain, may undermine their respect for the Bible and the teacher. This will be particularly so in the case of those who have no connection with Christianity outside the school; the difficulty does not arise for those whose views of the Bible coincide with those of the teacher.

It is probably more realistic to show them that the Christian search for truth is based on experience and that the Bible, properly used, can give guidance on the Christian interpretation of experience, but does not exempt us from making that interpretation. The Bible can then be seen as a true guide and not an intellectual tyrant. As Ruth Robinson has pointed out, 'Biblical truth is relevant to the child to the extent that it provides a definition or an explanation of what he already "knows", in the deepest sense, from experience' (J. A. T. Robinson: *The New Reformation?*).

The associative effect of the Bible on Christian thinking must also be taken into consideration. To Christians, who have regularly heard the Scriptures read in public worship, who have studied them 'devotionally' and who accept them as an authoritative source of revelation, Bible reading evokes many associated thoughts and memories, not all of them connected logically with the meaning of the passage being studied. C. H. Dodd has described this process in these words:

Most of us in this country today could say that whatever stands for religion to us has from our earliest days found expression in the speech of the Bible. No wonder that when we hear it read at the solemn assembly its words carry 'overtones' of association. Their precise meaning may not be present to us. They stir half-forgotten things in our subconscious minds, bred there partly by our explicit experience, partly by that which we have absorbed from our religious environment and tradition. Given certain conditions, religious feelings of real value may be evoked by such a use of the Scriptures even without clear understanding. . . . They owe their effect, not in the first place to their intelligible meaning, but to the 'aura' of sacred association surrounding them. (*The Authority of the Bible*; Nisbet, 1938, p. 4.)

This is also true to an extent in the classroom. For pupils with a Christian and church-going background, the reading of Bible stories may recall associated religious ideas learned elsewhere and be a religiously edifying and satisfying experience. It recalls and strengthens their favourable attitude to religion and so disposes them to accept the religious ideas the teacher seeks to put before them, and for these children a Bible-centred lesson will be effective. But to those who have met the Bible only in school, it can have no such evocative meaning, and can speak to them only in so far as they understand intellectually its statements, and find them acceptable. For these pupils it is not a rich source of religious thought but a collection of holy words, difficult thoughts and archaic language. Far from strengthening a favourable attitude, the study of it may have an opposite effect and be a means of impeding their religious learning, and for these pupils an 'experience-centred' approach may be more profitable.

THE NATURE OF THE BIBLE MATERIAL

The Bible is a collection of writings, set down at different times by writers whose motives were more complex than straightforward story telling. If it is to reveal its true meaning both the motives and the circumstances of the writers must be taken into consideration. Furthermore, account must be taken of the fact that the authors had a different philosophical outlook and method of expression from that normally used today. Some of the material needs sophisticated understanding and the teacher has to ask himself whether this is within the capabilities of his pupils. Not all of the Scriptures are equally difficult, but careful grading according to the complexity of understanding involved seems necessary. The present syllabuses attempt little of this apart from reserving the study of the prophets and the epistles for the older classes.

The Biblical material might profitably be classified thus:

1. Plain story telling, which can be easily understood at its face value. In fact there is very little of this material, although some of the stories in Acts and some of the more mundane parts of Hebrew history might be so described.

2. Stories in which events are described in the light of the writer's knowledge and with the symbols natural to his time, but which we might tell differently, e.g. stories which attribute illness to demon possession, and stories such as Jacob at Jabbok (*Genesis* **32**, 24-32) and Moses at the burning bush (*Exodus* **3**), which describe inner spiritual experiences as anthopormorphic conversations with God or as theophanies. Such material needs not only knowledge of the stories themselves, but also of the outlook and thought-forms of the writer and the insight to translate his statements into present day equivalents. It is doubtful whether children can do this, or even be helped to do it, until they have a developed historical sense and the ability to think abstractly about the nature of verbal communication.

3. Stories told to illustrate a religious belief or theory. Most of the historical narrative would come into this category, since it was written to show that God exercises a guiding and moral influence on history and, in order to make this point, the writers attribute more to direct divine intervention in human affairs than objective reporting would permit, e.g. the plagues (*Exodus* **7-12**), the escape of Paul at Phillippi (*Acts* **16**, 25-34), the crossing of the Red Sea (*Exodus* **14**), etc. Here again, full understanding demands awareness of how the presuppositions and purposes of a writer can influence his writings, which is not possible until some degree of abstract thinking is achieved.

4. Parable and edifying stories, both historical and fictional, in which the reader is intended to learn from the experiences related and apply the lesson to his own life, e.g. Jonah, Daniel and the lions (*Daniel* **6**, 10-23), Naaman the Syrian (*II Kings* **5**), the Prodigal Son (*Luke* **15**, 11-32), etc. There seems little difficulty in using this with wide age groups, provided the teacher is clear why he is using this material and freely admits that much of it is parable and that its religious value does not depend on its being accepted as history.

5. Allegory, e.g. the early *Genesis* stories and much of *St. John's Gospel*, which bear witness to some profound truth about the nature of God or about human nature, and the relation between the two. Such material needs some breadth of experience and ability to reflect upon it, as well as appreciation of allegorical expression, and probably cannot be used profitably much below sixth form level.

6. Poetry, of which the Psalms, David's lament over Saul and Jonathan (*II Samuel* **1**, 20-7), and the hymn to charity in *I Corinthians* **13** are obvious examples. This is intended to speak to the spirit and to the aesthetic sense, and might be used at any stage of religious education, provided the general meaning is within the capacity of the pupils. But the teacher must recognise clearly that he is using it as he would use other poetry, to train the aesthetic rather than the cognitive aspect of religion.

7. Theological statements, which tell directly of God's nature and purpose, of faith, and of man's religious duties. This is found most extensively in the Epistles and in the Decalogue (*Exodus* **20**, 1-17), and the Sermon on the Mount (*Matthew* **5-7**), but is also frequently to

be encountered in particular verses of the prophets, and the Gospels, e.g. *Micah* **6**, 8; *Matthew* **11**, 27; **18**, 35. These are of varying difficulty, depending on the profundity of thought involved rather than on the method of expression and one has to ask whether they are within the understanding of the pupil before introducing them into a lesson.

Many of these categories overlap, and not even Biblical scholars would always agree as to the assignment of many passages. Some teachers have views of the Bible which make such a critical appraisal repugnant and others, while sympathetic to the critical approach, are strangely hesitant to use it, either from fear of being thought unorthodox or of confusing the children. However, one would hope that the findings of Biblical and historical scholarship are now sufficiently widely accepted for it to be taken seriously in school teaching, and that means grading Bible material, according to its inherent difficulty and the complexity of understanding needed for the writer to convey his intended meaning, by some such scheme as that enumerated above. Having done this, it is necessary to ask at what stage of the child's development can each type of material meaningfully be presented to him. In doing this account must be taken of the way in which children understand Bible material.

CHILDREN'S UNDERSTANDING OF THE BIBLE

More knowledge of this subject is urgently needed. Systematic research over a wide area of Biblical material to show how children of different ages understand it is indicated. In general, however, it seems true that at the fairy-tale stage children regard Bible stories as they regard the stories of witches, fairies and magic which are told them, rejoicing in the story itself without seeking a deeper meaning or asking 'Is it true?' At the stage of concrete operational thinking, they understand stories in a literal way. The interpretation of allegory, the idea of stories told to illustrate a thesis or belief, and the understanding of the allowance that must be made for Bible stories coming from an age of different symbols and thought-forms, is impossible to them. They understand stories at their face value and are appreciative of them only as fact. They reject fairy stories at this time because they conflict with their widening experience. If Bible stories similarly conflict they do not reject them, because the Bible is supported by the authority of teacher and Church, and possibly parents. This is but a suspended judgment and religion, and the Bible stories in which it is conveyed, becomes the subject of special thinking, forming a fantasy world, divorced from ordinary experience, respected still, but not wholly believed. Persistent use of such stories in teaching, without an attempt to lead to a more subtle and spiritual understanding of them, may cause intolerable conflict in which the religious view of life is rejected and never recovered. The significant lessening of belief during secondary school age may be due to this. Use of Bible material which needs a maturer understanding than the pupil can bring to it, and failure to help him understand the true nature of that material when he can appreciate it, may cause him to cease thinking about religion by the time he has passed into the stage of abstract operational thought, and acquired the ability to think deeply and understandingly about it. Grading of the Bible material according to the complexity of understanding involved, and a matching of that material to the child's ability to comprehend it, would seem to be one of the pressing tasks of religious educators, even though many of the time-honoured and famous stories would not be used until a much older age than is customary. 'The recommendation may have to be faced that very little Biblical material is suitable before Secondary Schooling' (Goldman, *op. cit.*, p. 225).

With the foregoing in mind, we are able to consider the essential difference between a Bible-centred approach and a child-centred approach to religious education. The Bible-centred approach assumes that any study of the scriptures is beneficial and that, provided the vocabulary and the syntax are intelligible to him, every reader understands them in the same way. The child-centred approach recognises that when truth is expressed, not in the unambiguous formulae of the scientific text book, but in the imaginative and historical way that it is in the Bible, the presuppositions, the mental ability, and the previous experience of the reader condition and modify his understanding of what he reads. It therefore tries to fit the Bible to the child's understanding and not the child to the Bible. It takes account of the fact that church-going, Sunday school attending pupils may bring doctrinal beliefs and emotional associations to the study which gives the text a different meaning for them than for their fellows. It further recognises that some parts of the Bible need more complex understanding than others, and tries to select the passages most appropriate to the stage of thought that the pupils have reached. Naturally such an approach creates problems in classes where some are church-goers and others are not, and it demands on the part of the teacher both a closer sympathy with the pupil's mentality and a deeper knowledge of critical ideas of the Bible. In the earlier stages of education it may involve less direct use of the scriptures. It does not, however, mean a rejection of the Bible, or the ignoring of its message. Rather is it an attempt to free that message from misunderstanding due to the pupil's immaturity, to allow it to speak more directly to his experience and therefore to be accepted more intelligently and more permanently.

6

The strategy of religious education

One of the most fruitful concepts in recent educational thought has been that of 'readiness'. It recognises that there is an appropriate moment in child's development when he is ready to proceed to the next stage of learning. Thus there is a time of readiness for reading, readiness for number concept, and arrival at this moment of readiness depends on previous appropriate experience. The duty and art of the teacher is to prepare for that moment of readiness by providing the necessary experience, and to recognise when it is reached. To attempt to teach concepts before the child is ready for them is not only to invite failure but also to run the risk of inhibiting the child from acquiring the desired learning when it is possible to him. For instance, in arithmetic it is inadvisable to teach number concept until the child has had experience of numerical relationships in actual objects, for although he may acquire a mechanical facility for 'doing sums' he does not understand the concepts involved and this retards mathematical progress at a later time.

It is now being recognised that the idea of readiness can

be applied to religious education. Till the present little has been known about the psychological stages of religious growth, and it was assumed that children were religious in the same way at all ages. Religious education varied little in content or method between the upper infant school and the sixth form, with the result that in the earlier stages it was too abstract and in the later stages too elementary. The younger child appeared to acquire the appropriate religious concepts because he made the expected answers which he had learned verbally, but in the secondary school stage he ceased to do this and rejected religion and all its concepts as childish. Probably this was because he had never really understood the ideas placed before him, which eventually seemed to him boring and irrelevant. Thus he ceased to give his attention to them before he became able to understand them.

A rethinking of the strategy of the subject would therefore seem necessary. We have to ask, 'What religious understanding is possible for a child in his present state of development?; What experience and mental ability are needed to allow him to proceed to the next phase of understanding?; What type of teaching will enable him to pass easily and naturally to that following phase?'. The end product will all the while be kept in mind, and the process of religious education viewed as a whole. The eventual aim is that the school leaver will have sufficient knowledge to make a serious and informed decision about religion, but he can reach this position only by passing through a series of connected stages, in each of which his understanding is fragmentary and incomplete. The subject needs a succession of phased aims, each designed to bring the child to the experience and understanding appropriate to his age, with the recognition that much of the early training may not closely approximate to what is generally regarded as formal religious education. There follows an attempt to outline a programme of phased religious education.

THE INFANT SCHOOL

Formal religious education is inappropriate in early childhood. At this stage philosophical and theological ideas are quite beyond the pupil and ultimate questions will not trouble him. He is still discovering the nature of the world in which he lives and wondering at it. Perhaps the most that religious education can do is to help him to rejoice in the beauty and mystery to be found in creation, and to give him the experience of love and kindliness and goodness on which more mature theological concepts are based. This can be done quite as well in lessons of nature and discovery and art as in specific scripture lessons, and the latter may have little profit at this age. Specific religious teaching may result in little more than incomprehended orthodox responses and misunderstanding. R. S. Lee has discussed this in his *Your Growing Child and Religion* (1965):

> The young child of this age is still incapable of understanding religious ideas and notions, but to unwary parents or teachers he may seem to be understanding them while all the time he has misunderstood them, giving them his own interpretation. He may say his 'prayers', talk about God, sing the hymns he is taught, and so on, giving the actual appearance of being religious, but to the child what he does has another significance altogether. It may be just an interesting game, playing at being grown up, or just something to please

Father or Mother or teacher. . . . If pressure is brought upon him, either by accidents or circumstances or by deliberate effort on the part of his parents, to try to make him religious in the adult sense, he is likely to become fixed in his infantile understanding. The ideas and feelings he has about these new activities will be overdeveloped by the emphasis put upon them, making it difficult for him to pass smoothly out of them in the way to truer understanding of what religion is. (p. 126)

Infant school children will inevitably hear the word God and meet such statements as ' God is father of all' and 'God is living' and be led to ask 'What is God like?' and some attempt must be made to reply to such questions honestly. Answers in theological terms are likely to lead to confusion rather than comprehension and it may be wiser to appeal to experience by some such words as 'God looks after us like a good father' or 'God is the name grown-ups give to all that is good and beautiful in the world'. The important thing is to present a favourable attitude to the idea of God, so that the child will realise there is more to be learned and will go on learning as his widening experience permits (see Lee, *op. cit.*, pp. 130-6). Indeed the presentation and strengthening of the idea of wonder and goodness in the world, and of a favourable attitude to a religious explanation of life and its setting, is all that can and ought to be attempted during infant schooling.

THE JUNIOR SCHOOL

In the junior school the pupil has reached a maturer understanding and is beginning to think operationally rather than instinctively, but still in terms of the concrete and the particular. Three aspects of his development are relevant for religious development. Firstly, he is beginning to recognise personal relationships and the problems of living together with others; secondly, he is collecting innumerable facts about the world, and thirdly he is forming attitudes to ideas and institutions which are going greatly to influence his future learning about them. These three things indicate the lines of religious teaching at this stage.

(*a*) *Understanding personal relationships.* By junior school age children have begun to break out of the narrower experience of home and self to begin to make contact with their peers through games and gangs. They have experience of friendship and childish enmities, and have started to realise that living with others involves problems of personal relationships and some modification of spontaneous behaviour. Proper management of such relationships are the concern of the Christian religion, the second commandment of which is 'Thou shalt love thy neighbour as thyself'. Consideration of them is part of Junior School religious education, and Bible stories which deal with the relationship of man to man—e.g. Joseph and his brothers (*Genesis* **37-45**), Jacob and Esau (*Genesis* **27**, **32** and **33**), Peter's denial (*Luke* **23**, 54-61), the Good Samaritan (*Luke* **10**, 30-7) can be read and discussed. Older junior school pupils, especially the most intelligent quicker developers, will be acquiring deeper religious susceptibilities and be able to learn something of man's relationship with God which is the basis of the first Christian commandment 'Thou shalt love the Lord thy God'. Bible stories which tell of this e.g. Abraham's sacrifice (*Genesis* **22**, 1-14), Jacob's ladder (*Genesis* **28**, 10-17) and the parable of the talents (*Matthew* **25**, 14-19) can be taught, although care must be taken to disentangle it from its metaphorical expression, as in the case of the second example quoted.

(b) Acquiring factual knowledge. Though the pupil cannot reason abstractly, some knowledge of facts will be needed as a basis of this theoretical reasoning at a later date. The Junior School is the place to acquire factual knowledge and pupils absorb facts easily at this time and find in them some security, since facts are unchanging and unquestionable. Bible stories which are plain straightforward historical stories make good teaching material. So too does the writing, transmission and translation of the Bible text. Some knowledge of the chronology of Bible events will not be out of place and may prevent in the future confused thinking similar to that shown by the secondary school pupil who wrote 'Moses was a good Christian'. The main events of Christian history, such as the coming of Christianity to Britain, the nature of Church buildings and furnishings, and information about the Christian contribution to social work provide further material. The criterion to be applied in selection is that the lesson should contain facts of an empirical nature and not include symbolic representation of beliefs which the child may at this age mistake for empirical fact and have to reinterpret at a later date.

(c) The inculcation of favourable attitudes. Hyde has shown that learning in the secondary school is dependent on a favourable attitude (see chapter 3, p. 49), and one of the contributions of the Junior School would seem to be the imparting of favourable attitudes. This raises the question of how attitudes are inculcated. They are frequently transmitted by actions, gestures and stray remarks, at home and in the playground as well as in the lessons.

The teacher may be daunted by the consideration that the pupil is exposed to many attitudes in out-of-school hours which will frustrate his best efforts. Yet there are a number of things the teacher can do which influence the children's attitudes. Finally his own attitudes will, almost unconsciously, be transferred to them by the way he presents his lesson and the enthusiasm he shows for his subject. Perhaps this justifies the demand that only sincerely religious people should teach the subject, provided they have sufficiently wide sympathy as to understand pupils with non-religious backgrounds.

Further, as Hyde again has demonstrated, 'knowledge about' and 'favourable attitude to' the subject go hand in hand, and therefore much of the factual knowledge advocated above, will strengthen the desired attitudes. Visits to local churches (not necessarily for services) and a natural contact with the clergy and ministers attached to them can help, but how far these are possible depends on the type of school, the prevailing tradition, and the condition, both architectural and spiritual, of these churches.

Perhaps the most important factor in attitude development is that the pupils should feel personally involved in the subject. Where the teaching is a formal presentation of stories of a remote age, frequently already heard all too often, boredom must eventually arise. This can be avoided by giving the class practical work, something to do or make, of which they can feel possessive and proud. The making of a picture, frieze or chart, to which all the class, however inartistic, contribute a drawing, and which they can show school-fellows and visiting parents is one method of doing this. The influence of the morning assembly in attitude formation needs also to be considered. Where this is a dull and formal procedure, from which attention can easily be withdrawn, unfavourable attitudes to religion must result, and the practice of involving the children by allowing them frequently to plan and take part in the assembly and the relating of it to things that happen in the neighbourhood and to events heard on the radio and television might profitably be extended. If, by the time he leaves the Junior School, the pupil has some idea of the significance of personal relationships, some fair knowledge of the empirical facts of how religion is expressed and organised, and a favourable attitude to it, he is ready, and like as not willing, to advance to the next stage, which is thinking, with genuine insight about its essential nature.

EARLY SECONDARY SCHOOL YEARS

The years from 11 to 14 can be the most formative ones in the development of a religious view of life. This is the time when abstract thinking becomes possible and spiritual experience begins to be explored. The latter frequently shows itself, especially in boys, with a temporary period of religious activity, but this can quickly be succeeded by a period of hard determinism in which the religion lately held is entirely jettisoned.

What is happening is that they are beginning to replace formal observance and acceptance with a truly religious feeling in depth. It is with such experience as this that the Bible is concerned. But since it is inward and wholly personal it can be expressed only in symbol and story, and it should be the aim of religious teaching to point this out, and help pupils to understand what the Bible is really saying, and to show how its characters were having experiences similar in quality to those which they are feeling for the first time. If this is not done they begin to look on the Bible as a collection of incredible stories and make a distinction between the 'religion' that is taught, and the true religion that they are feeling.

The aim at this stage, then, is to help pupils to recognise spiritual experience and its expression in the Bible and to accord it respect. Perhaps it would be as well if the Bible were rarely read before this time and the bulk of its teaching introduced at this age. Even if most children have already encountered a number of Bible stories elsewhere it is advisable to work through much of the text systematically with a different approach. The purpose is not to tell again the story, but to ask of it 'What is the Bible writer really trying to say?; What spiritual experience is told here in symbol and parabolic story?'. The present writer would advocate that a thorough-going critical, and even radical, approach, making use of all available Biblical scholarship, should be employed, while recognising that many teachers will feel unable to agree.

Since Goldman has provided information of how children think of the narrative of Moses and the burning bush, when exposed to uncritical teaching, perhaps this may serve as an example of what is intended. On the face of it the story tells of an ever-burning fire from which God held an audible conversation with Moses. Younger children accept this without demur, but by early adolescence they are beginning to think about it rationally, and to argue that ever-burning fires are impossible, and that no one ever seems to have heard God speak audibly out of one, and that probably such an experience is also impossible. They begin to doubt the historicity of the story, and, by association, many other things that religious people say. To retell the story is to reinforce doubts rather than belief. It has quite a different effect if it is admitted that the narrative is a literary device to enable us to know what was going on in Moses' mind. His enslaved compatriots in Egypt needed a leader to organise their escape. He had been trained as a leader by virtue of being reared in Pharaoh's palace, but was neglecting his education and having an easy time in Midian. This gave him a bad conscience. A fire symbolised in contemporary thought the presence of God, and when Moses sees a strange fire (there seems no harm in admitting that, in an oil-bearing region, it was probably a 'gusher') he feels God near and begins to pray. The subject of his prayer is his uneasy conscience and he becomes convinced God wants him to return and use his talents and training to free his fellow countrymen. Taught in that way, the story links up with the children's experience, for they too have times of doubt and uneasy conscience. It shows them that God speaks, not in voices from supernatural phenomena, but in the soul, through the pattern of experience, and that the realisation of his guidance is what we call prayer.

In a similar way the account of Elijah at Mt. Carmel (*I Kings* **19**, 4-16), Isaiah in the Temple (*Isaiah* **6**, 1-8), the Baptism and Temptation of Jesus (*Matthew* **3**, 13 to **4**, 11), the Pentecost (*Acts* **2**, 1-4), and the conversion of St. Paul (*Acts* **9**, 1-9) can be presented in such a way as to help children to understand and deepen their own religious aspirations, so that they continue to take them seriously, and are ready to proceed to the next stage, which is the discussion of their nature and value.

LATER SECONDARY SCHOOL YEARS

Just as the fancies of appetite give a clue to the diet the

body needs, so the demands of adolescents for a certain type of teaching can give guidance to the sort of religious education that will be helpful to them. At the moment the demand in the final years at school is for discussion rather than formal teaching. This ought to be taken seriously, for it is based on a conviction that a man's religion must be the result of his own experience, and is a personal thing that he must find for himself, not something to be imposed on him from without. The aim of religious education at this stage is to help the students to find the beliefs and values that are going to be real and imperative to them. This can be done by discussion and those who hold that there are certain objective truths and values that are valid for all men everywhere can be sufficiently confident of them to think that properly ordered discussion will bring them to light.

The problem is how to achieve properly ordered discussion and a systematic education through it. At its worst a class discussion can be little more than a series of inconclusive and ill-informed wrangles. Loukes has called it 'anti-syllabus' and 'anti-method' (*op. cit.*, p. 143). It probably needs more planning beforehand and control during the lesson than formal methods, but if the teacher gives it sufficient forethought there is no reason why it should not yield results. There are three main problems connected with the discussion method, namely, how to make it systematically cover a coherent syllabus, how to control its course in the classroom, and how to lead it to an explicit conclusion, while at the same time leaving it free enough to be a genuine discussion.

If a series of discussions are to form a systematic education it is insufficient for the teacher to enter the classroom, to say, 'Well, what shall we talk about today?' and then to allow the conversation to wander where it will. He must plan what ground is to be covered by discussion during a term or a year, listing the topics to be discussed. There is no need to be rigid about the order, for often a contemporary event, a newspaper report, or a television programme will make one of those topics immediately relevant, and it can be introduced while the opportunity is there. It is as well to remember that many subjects of a semi-religious nature are discussed in other lessons, and that in some schools the students get tired of a diet of sex, colour-bar and nuclear disarmament. Topicality need not be the only directing factor, and some teachers have found that a series of discussions on the Ten Commandments and the articles of the Apostles creed have been welcomed and found helpful. The main necessity, however, is that there shall be a syllabus for the discussions.

In the classroom the teacher must control the lesson without stifling spontaneous contributions. He needs to think in advance what aspects of the subject ought to be covered and how much time can be allocated to each, and must be prepared to ask the class to move on and consider the subject from a new angle. This will enable him to ask the opinions of those who have not contributed so far, and to draw them into the discussion. A black-board summary of the points covered can structure the discussion and help the class to see the progress being made. As well as chairing the lesson in this way, the teacher will provide information when needed, and correct the misinformation that is often volunteered. Should his own opinion be asked, as frequently it will, he can give it, provided he permits it to be criticised as freely as any other opinion. If he controls the discussion along these lines it need not degenerate into the blind and vociferous leading the blind and the dumb.

There remains the need to reach some kind of conclusion at the end of the lesson. The teacher himself can give a summary and state the points decided, but there is the danger that he will appear to be 'putting the class right' and forcing on them a predetermined conclusion. If he is in fact doing this, it will be resented and inhibit free discussion in later classes. With most intelligent students it is possible to ask one of them to summarise the lesson, giving him warning, so that he can be noting the course of the conversation and its decision. Perhaps the best method of all, if time permits, is for the class to write an essay on the topic, each member giving his personal point of view. The virtue of such writing is that all the class has to think about the subject and make a decision about it.

The discussion method is no sinecure for the teacher. But if by the methods mentioned above, or by others which he discovers for himself, he can make the discussions systematic, progressive, focussed, and conclusive as far as the subject permits, it can help students, provided they have been given the right attitudes and information in earlier years, to come to a sincere and informed personal decision about religious questions, about conduct, and about the nature and purpose of life, which is the ultimate aim of religious education.

Such a scheme of phased religious education has the merit of taking into account recent theological thought, the information that research has provided of how children understand religious concepts, and the widely accepted results of Biblical criticism. However, it has certain defects.

One objection to it is that it leads to definite religious knowledge only in middle adolescence and provides no guidance for the younger child. Does he not need a religion suited to his understanding? One wonders if he does, and whether adults do not project onto children their own mature questions and needs. Provided he is given adequate guidance on conduct and manners, the young child does not ask heart-searching questions of a philosophical nature, even when faced with some of the tragedies of life, and if he did he would not be able to understand the answers. Such problems do arise however in adolescence and the type of religious education outlined may then help him to discover some of the answers for himself.

It might further be said that the training envisaged is in the cognitive aspects of religion only and tends to ignore its emotional and aesthetic elements. Yet it is in its cognitive aspects that religious education is weakest. The problems of belief at present are intellectual problems of the relation of the spiritual view of life to the material and causative explanations of scientific exploration, and the nature of value judgments. Because religion in its traditional expression often seems at variance with the intellectual climate of the age, it is rejected unexamined and misunderstood by many before their education is complete. A religious education which does not examine the intellectual justifications for belief is unlikely to meet with permanent success.

In an era of religious certainty it is possible for religious education to be the transmission of an accepted body of doctrine, known by the teacher and to be learned by the pupil. At the present time of uncertainty and rethinking it must be a search in which teacher and student 'feel after truth and find it', as far as their experience and understanding allow. But it is a search based on the belief that the past experience of the human race can provide helpful signposts, that honest thinking can lead to truth, and that life has been given us with point and purpose by a personal power greater than man, and is therefore not 'a tale told by an idiot, full of sound and fury, signifying nothing'.

Suggestions for further reading

1. Books dealing with recent trends in theological thinking:

TILLICH, P.: *The Shaking of the Foundations.* Pelican Books, 1962.
A series of essays and sermons, which have been influential in causing theologians to rethink the effectiveness of the symbols in which the Christian faith has been traditionally expressed.

ROBINSON, J. A. T.: *Honest to God.* S.C.M. Press, 1963.
A popular exposition of the ideas of Tillich, as well as those of Bultmann and Bonhoeffer.

ROBINSON, J. A. T.: *The New Reformation?* S.C.M. Press, 1965.
A sequel to *Honest to God,* which aims to be more definite and constructive. Includes a perceptive essay by Ruth Robinson on the teaching of religion to young children.

LLOYD, R.: *The Ferment in the Church.* S.C.M. Press, 1964.
An attempt to describe the practical effect that the ideas popularised by Robinson will have on the belief and organisation of the Christian Churches.

2. Books dealing with the manner in which children's religious beliefs develop:

GOLDMAN, R. J.: *Religious Thinking from Childhood to Adolescence.* Routledge & Kegan Paul, 1964.

An account of a careful research into the understanding children have of religious ideas at various ages, and radical suggestions for the revision of syllabus and methods in the light of the findings. A large and important book.

GOLDMAN, R. J.: *Readiness for Religion*. Routledge & Kegan Paul. 1965.

Summarises, in more popular form, the main findings of Dr. Goldman's research, and discusses more fully its application in the classroom. Not to be confused with the 'Readiness for Religion' series, edited by Dr. Goldman and published by Rupert Hart-Davis, which consists of work cards for pupils in the Primary School and lower Secondary School. To some extent it is the teacher's handbook to these.

HYDE, K. E.: *Religious Learning in Adolescence*. Published for the University of Birmingham Institute of Education by Oliver and Boyd, 1965.

A concise account of a research done among Secondary Modern School children, dealing chiefly with the influence of attitude upon learning.

LEE, R. S.: *Your Growing Child and Religion*. Pelican Books, 1965.

An outline of the growth of a child's mind and personality from the earliest stages, and of the influences that evoke in it a religious consciousness.

MADGE, V.: *Children in Search of Meaning*. S.C.M. Press, 1965.

A record of the ways in which Primary School children seek for meaning in their experience, and can be led to find the religious meaning of it. Based on careful observation and research.

YEAXLEE, B. A.: *Religion and the Growing Mind*. Nisbet, 1939.

Written long before the present rethinking of Religious Education began, it still contains many useful insights, especially into the way in which parents and teachers, irrespective of their own beliefs, unconsciously influence children's religious development.

3. Books dealing with the social background to religious education:

JEFFREYS, M. V. C.: *Personal Values in the Modern World.*
Pelican Books, 1962.

A discussion of the need to rediscover a coherent view of experience, and the part that education can play in this.

NIBLETT, W. R.: *Christian Education in a Secular Society.*
O.U.P., 1960.

An examination of the practical tasks and objectives of Christian teachers in secondary schools in terms of their school situation, and in the wider contemporary social setting. It deals with this in terms of other subjects, as well as religious education.

Ed. NIBLETT, W. R.: *Moral Education in a Changing Society.*
Faber & Faber, 1963.

A series of lectures by various speakers, some with religious views, some agnostic, concerning the need for moral education and the problems that it involves.

4. Books dealing with religious education:

HILLIARD, F. H.: *The Teacher and Religion.* James Clarke, 1963.

An experienced book, surveying a wide field, dealing, among other things, with the educational approach to religious education, and the outlook and qualifications necessary to those who undertake it.

LOUKES, H.: *Teenage Religion.* S.C.M. Press, 1961.

Now almost a classic, this book contains many quotations from secondary modern school pupils, which reveal their understanding, and more frequent misunderstanding of what they have been taught. It discusses the problems raised, and suggests ways a teacher can use their genuine interest in 'real life' situations.

LOUKES, H.: *New Ground in Christian Education.* S.C.M. Press, 1965.

This covers much the same ground as *Teenage Religion*, but at greater depth, and is based on a piece of research rather than on random comments. It is highly readable, and argues that effective teaching starts from day to day experience and leads the pupils to a personal insight into its meaning.

SUGGESTIONS FOR FURTHER READING

ACLAND, R.: *We Teach Them Wrong*. Gollancz, 1963.

A critical examination of secondary school religious education, with some suggestions as to how it might be improved. The author's thought is as much coloured by his experience as a practical politician as by his time as a teacher, and the result is often stimulating if not always systematic.

DEWAR, D.: *Backward Christian Soldiers*. Hutchinson, 1964.

Mrs. Dewar writes as a parent and a journalist. She has collected her facts and written them down with the speed and facility associated with newspaper articles, and the 'experts' she consults are not those generally connected with religious education. But the book is often thought-provoking and gives the point of view of an intelligent but puzzled parent.

Date Due

FE 28 72			
APR 2 7 1996			